THE ROYAL SHAKESPEARE COMPANY

The Royal Shakespeare Company is one of t

The Company is widely regarded as one of the most important interpreters of Shakespeare and other classical dramatists. Today the RSC is at the leading edge of classical theatre, with an international reputation for artistic excellence, accessibility and high-quality live performance.

Our mission at the RSC is to create outstanding theatre that is relevant to our times through the work of Shakespeare, other Renaissance dramatists, European theatre and new plays. We aim to attract and inspire the best artists, and to sustain and delight audiences of all ages throughout the world.

This year RSC productions in Stratford-upon-Avon are performed over two seasons: the main Summer Festival Season and a shorter Winter Season. Large-scale productions of the plays of Shakespeare, other classical theatre and Christmas family shows are performed in the Royal Shakespeare Theatre, the Company's main house. The galleried Swan Theatre offers a closer relationship between actors and audience. Productions in the Swan Theatre include work by both classic and contemporary dramatists. The Other Place, the Company's studio theatre, explores Elizabethan and Jacobean theatre alongside experimental and new work.

The Other Place also houses special developmental projects and some of the RSC's education work, including the annual Prince of Wales Shakespeare School.

The Company's roots in Stratford-upon-Avon stretch back to the nineteenth century. However, since the 1960s, the RSC's work in Stratford has been complemented by a regular presence in London.

But Stratford and London are only part of the story. Twenty-five years of residency in the city of Newcastle-upon-Tyne have forged a strong link between RSC artists and audiences in the North-East. Many of our productions also visit major regional theatres around Britain. And our annual regional tour sets up its own travelling auditorium in community centres, sport halls and schools in towns throughout the UK without access to professional theatre.

While the UK is the Company's home, our audiences are global. The Company regularly plays to enthusiastic audiences in other parts of Europe, across the United States, the Americas, Asia and Australasia. The RSC is proud of its relationships with partnering organisations in other countries, particularly in America.

Despite continual change, the RSC today is still at heart an ensemble company, and the continuation of this great tradition informs the work of all its members. Directors, actors, dramatists and theatre practitioners all collaborate in the creation of the RSC's distinctive and unmistakable approach to theatre.

THE OTHER PLACE

The Other Place is the RSC's smallest theatre. The theatre also houses our rehearsal studios and has a central role in the history of the RSC as a centre for research and development.

Our roots lie in two distinct areas. In the early 1960s Michel St Denis brought to the company the European tradition of 'the actors' laboratory' and worked with actors, directors, writers, designers and technical staff to develop singly and together their own craft and imagination and that of the company.

While the company continued to explore ways of revealing Elizabethan drama, actors and directors sought new audiences for new work. Theatregoround was born. This was the first small-scale work the company had done and it laid the foundation for subsequent seasons at The Roundhouse and The Place in London. The 'tin hut' became The Other Place and Buzz Goodbody its first artistic director. In 1991 we outgrew the tin hut and moved to our present purpose-built home.

This season we celebrate our tenth anniversary in this theatre with the production of three new plays. David Edgar and Peter Whelan continue their long association with the RSC and Martin McDonagh joins them to complete our trilogy of new writing for the new century.

Steven Pimlott
Director of The Other Place

Since its inception The Other Place has produced work by many of the major contemporary dramatists: Edward Bond, Howard Brenton, Nick Dear, Peter Flannery, Christopher Hampton, Mike Leigh, David Rudkin, Willy Russell, Charles Wood, and more recently, Biyi Bandele, April de Angelis, Anne Devlin, Pam Gems, Robert Holman, Bernard-Marie Koltés, Derek Walcott, and Nigel Williams. This season our current exhibition in the café reflects this unique body of new writing.

Alongside these the classical balance has been maintained with new productions of European classics and Shakespeare. As well as new plays in performance, we run workshops with young writers, giving them the chance to work with RSC actors on themes which reflect the concerns of the classical repertoire.

In the present-day TOP we remember Buzz Goodbody and Michel St Denis in the rehearsal rooms named after them and their legacy continues in our developmental work. Each year we work with actors to assemble a programme of workshops focusing on different disciplines. We are members of the Union of European Theatres and RSC actors, directors and designers regularly meet their European counterparts for an exchange of ideas.

THE ROYAL SHAKESPEARE COMPANY

RSC EDUCATION AND COLLECTIONS

The objective of the RSC Education Department is to enable as many people as possible, from all walks of life, to have easy access to the great works of Shakespeare, the Renaissance and the theatre.

To do this, we are building a team which supports the productions that the Company presents onstage for the general public, special interest groups and for education establishments of all kinds.

We are also planning to develop our contribution as a significant learning resource in the fields of Shakespeare, the Renaissance, classical and modern theatre, theatre arts and the RSC. This resource is made available in many different ways, including workshops, teachers' programmes, summer courses, a menu of activities offered to group members of the audience, pre- and post-show events as part of the Events programme, open days, tours of the theatre, community activities, youth programmes and loans of parts of the RSC Collection for exhibitions and youth programmes. The RSC Collections, moved into a new home, will be used to create new programmes of learning and an expanded exhibition schedule.

We are developing the educational component of our new website to be launched this year. The RSC will make use of appropriate new technologies to disseminate its work in many different ways to its many audiences.

We can also use our knowledge of theatre techniques to help in other aspects of learning: classroom teaching techniques for subjects other than drama or English, including management and personnel issues.

Not all of these programmes are available all the time, and not all of them are yet in place. However, if you are interested in pursuing any of these options, the telephone numbers and e-mail addresses are as follows:

For information on general education activities contact the Education Administrator, Sarah Keevill on **01789 403462**, or e-mail her on **sarah.keevill @rsc.org.uk**.

To find out about backstage tours, please contact our Tour Manager, Anne Tippett on **01789 403405**, or e-mail her on **theatre.tours@rsc.org.uk**.

JOIN THE RSC

Associate and Overseas

For £8 a year you can become an RSC Associate Member. Benefits include:

* Advance information and priority booking for our Stratford and London Seasons (plus the Newcastle Season if you live in the appropriate area).
* Special priority booking subscription scheme for the Stratford Summer Festival season.
* Deferred payment facilities on Stratford tickets booked during the priority period (by instalments with a credit card).
* Special Members' performances for some Stratford and London productions.
* No fees payable on ticket re-sales in Stratford.
* Free RSC magazine.

Full members

For £24 all of the Associate benefits, plus:

* Guaranteed seats for RSC productions in the Royal Shakespeare Theatre, Swan Theatre and Barbican Theatre (for tickets booked during the priority period).
* An extra week of priority booking for Stratford and London seasons.
* 10% discount on purchases from RSC Shops.

Group and **Education** membership also available.

Overseas Members

The RSC tours regularly overseas. In recent years we've toured the USA, South America, Japan, India and Pakistan, as well as most parts of Europe. Wherever you are in the world, you can become an RSC Member. Overseas Membership is available from £15.

Special Overseas Members

All of the benefits of a Full Member, plus:

* A complimentary programme for each Royal Shakespeare Theatre production.

You will find application forms in the theatre foyers, or contact us at: Membership Office, Royal Shakespeare Theatre, Stratford-upon-Avon CV37 6BB or telephone **01789 403440**.

STAY IN TOUCH

For up-to-date news on the RSC, our productions and education work, visit the RSC's official web site: **www.rsc.org.uk**. Information on RSC performances is also available on Teletext.

On Ch4 p430

A PARTNERSHIP WITH THE RSC

The RSC is immensely grateful for the valuable support of its corporate sponsors and individual and charitable donors. Between them these groups provide up to £6m a year for the RSC and support a range of initiatives such as actor training, education workshops and access to our performances for all members of society.

The RSC is renowned throughout the world as one of the finest arts brands. A corporate partnership offers unique and creative opportunities both nationally and internationally, and benefits from our long and distinguished record of maintaining and developing relationships. Reaching over one million theatregoers a year, our Corporate Partnership programme progresses from Corporate Membership to Business Partnership to Season Sponsor to Title Sponsor, and offers the following benefits: extensive crediting and association; prestigious corporate hospitality; marketing and promotional initiatives; corporate citizenship and business networking opportunities. Our commitment to education, new writing and access provides a diverse portfolio of projects which offer new and exciting ways to develop partnerships which are non-traditional and mutually beneficial.

As an individual you may wish to support the work of the RSC through membership of the RSC Patrons. For as little as £21 per month you can join a cast drawn from our audience and the worlds of theatre, film, politics and business. Alternatively, the gift of a legacy to the RSC would enable the Company to maintain and increase new artistic and educational work with children and adults through our Acting and Education Funds.

For information about corporate partnership with the RSC, please contact Victoria Okotie,
Head of Corporate Partnerships,
Barbican Theatre, London EC2Y 8BQ.
Tel: **020 7382 7281**.
e-mail: **victoria.okotie@rsc.org.uk**

For information about individual relationships with the RSC, please contact Graeme Williamson,
Development Manager,
Royal Shakespeare Theatre, Waterside,
Stratford-upon-Avon CV37 6BB.
Tel: **01789 412661**.
e-mail: **graemew@rsc.org.uk**.

You can visit our web site at
www.rsc.org.uk/development.

The Prisoner's Dilemma was first performed by the Royal Shakespeare Company
at The Other Place, Stratford-upon-Avon, on 11 July 2001,
supported by RSC Platinum Corporate Members
The cast was as follows:

Douglas Rao	Al Bek/Young Man
Diana Kent	Floss
David Wilmot	James/2nd Drozhdan/2nd Paramilitary
Joseph Mydell	Patterson/Len
Penny Downie	Gina/Mother
Larry Lamb	Tom/Father
Trevor Cooper	Nikolai/Lou
Alex Zorbas	Waiter/1st Drozhdan/2nd Orderly/Trevelyan/Bodyguard/ Zelim/1st Paramilitary
Zoe Waites	Kelima
George Clarke/Joshua Dale	Jan/Boy/Aslan
Alan David	Erik/Yuri Vasilevich
Robert Bowman	Roman/2nd Kavkhazian Soldier
Robert Jezek	Hasim/1st Kavkhazian Soldier
Hattie Morahan	Emela/1st Orderly/Sailor/Translator

Directed by	**Michael Attenborough**
Designed by	**Es Devlin**
Lighting designed by	**Howard Harrison**
Music by	**Paddy Cunneen**
Fights by	**Terry King**
Sound designed by	**John A. Leonard for Aura**
Video and Animation by	**Gary Vernon**
Assistant Director	**Samantha Potter**
Translators and Foreign Language Advisors	**Helen Rappaport, Kevin Smith and Tiia Tempakka**
Dialect Coach	**Charmian Hoare**
Company voice work by	**RSC Voice Department**
Production Manager	**Mark Graham**
Costume Supervisor	**Fizz Jones**

Stage Manager	**Katie Vine**
Deputy Stage Manager	**Klare Roger**
Assistant Stage Manager	**Marisa Ferguson**

This production is supported by
Bacon and Woodrow, The British Land Company plc, LDV

DAVID EDGAR

David Edgar was born in 1948 into a theatre family. After a period in journalism, he took up writing full time in 1972. In 1989, he founded Britain's first graduate playwriting course, at the University of Birmingham, of which he was director for ten years. He was appointed as Britain's first Professor of Playwriting in 1995.

His original stage plays include *Death Story* (Birmingham Repertory Theatre, 1972), *Entertaining Strangers* (Dorchester Community Play, 1985, then National Theatre 1987), *That Summer* (Hampstead Theatre, London, 1987) and *The Shape of the Table* (National Theatre 1990). His stage adaptations include Albie Sachs's *Jail Diary* (Royal Shakespeare Company, 1978), Mary Barnes and Joe Berke's *Mary Barnes* (Birmingham Rep then Royal Court, London, 1978-9), a multi-award-winning version of Dickens's *Nicholas Nickleby* (Royal Shakespeare Company in London and New York, 1980-1, subsequently Channel 4), Stevenson's *Dr Jekyll and Mr Hyde* (Royal Shakespeare Company, 1991 and then Birmingham Rep, 1996) and Gitta Sereny's *Albert Speer* (National Theatre, 2000). His original plays for the RSC are *Destiny* (1976), *Maydays* (1983) and *Pentecost* (1994-5), which won, respectively, the John Whiting Award, the *Plays and Players* play of the year award, and the *Evening Standard* best play award.

David Edgar's television work includes the three-part serial *Vote for Them* (written with Neil Grant, BBC2, 1989), the single play *Buying a Landslide* (BBC2, 1992) and *Citizen Locke* (Channel Four, 1994). His radio work for the BBC includes *Talking to Mars* (1996) and and an adaptation of Eve Brook's novel *The Secret Parts* (2000). He also wrote the film *Lady Jane* for Paramount (1986). He writes and reviews for a wide variety of journals, including the *Guardian*, the *New Statesman* and the *London Review of Books*. He has published a volume of essays (*The Second Time as Farce*, 1988), and he edited and introduced a book on contemporary playwriting, *State of Play*, published in 1999.

Also by David Edgar

Albert Speer

Destiny

Entertaining Strangers

The Jail Diary of Albie Sachs

Mary Barnes

Nicholas Nickleby

Pentecost

Teendreams & Our Own People

That Summer

The Shape of the Table

Wreckers

Vote for Them

The Second Time as Farce

State of Play (*editor and introduction*)

David Edgar

THE PRISONER'S DILEMMA

NICK HERN BOOKS
London
www.nickhernbooks.co.uk

A Nick Hern Book

The Prisoner's Dilemma first published in 2001 as an original
paperback by Nick Hern Books Limited, 14 Larden Road,
London W3 7ST, in association with the Royal Shakespeare
Company, Barbican Centre, London EC2Y 8BQ

The Prisoner's Dilemma © 2001 by David Edgar

David Edgar has asserted his right to be identified as
the author of this work

Typeset by Country Setting, Kingsdown, Kent CT14 8ES
Printed and bound in Great Britain by Biddles, Guildford

A CIP catalogue record for this book is available from
the British Library

ISBN 185459 631 4

To Clarissa Brown

Acknowledgements

I am obligated to Helen Rappaport, Kevin Smith and Tiia
Tempakka who translated and taught the languages used in
the play.

For research help I am grateful to Lawrence Freedman of
King's College, London; Scilla Elworthy of the Oxford
Research Group; Hugh Miall of the University of Lancaster;
Peter Paul van der Groote of Médecin sans Frontières; and
the staff and graduate students of the University of Bradford's
Department of Peace Studies (including Nick Lewer, Sarah
Perrigo, Tom Woodhouse, Oliver Ramsbotham, Donna
Parkhurst, Tamara Duffey, Pia Johannson and Barbara Weber).
For further help and advice I am grateful to Penny Cherns,
Stephanie Dale, Charlotte Keatley, Ted Braun, Clarissa Brown,
Esther Richardson, Hilary Norrish, Kaite O'Reilly, Levan
Khetaguri, and David Sakvarelidze.

I owe a particular debt to David Kennedy of the Harvard Law
School, who introduced me to the function and practice of
role-play in international diplomacy (and much else besides);
and to Nigel Howard, whose concept of drama-theory was
crucial to the structuring of the play.

Much of the first act of *The Prisoner's Dilemma* began life as
a libretto written for the Stephen Oliver award. Titled *The
Bridge*, the opera was set by Tim Benjamin and presented at
the Royal Northern College of Music and the Covent Garden
Festival in 1998.

Finally, the quotations before and after the acts of the play are
drawn from Shakespeare, various television and press reports,
and the following books: *Contemporary Conflict Resolution*
(Hugh Miall, Oliver Ramsbotham, Tom Woodhouse, 1999),
The Clash of Civilizations and the Remaking of World Order
(Samuel P. Huntington, 1996), *Getting to Yes* (Roger Fisher
and William Ury, 1981), *Games, Threats and Treaties*

(Jon Hovi, 1998), *The Fight for Peace* (Eamonn Mallie and David McKittrick, 1996), *Gaza First* (Jane Corbin, 1994) and *Chechnya: Calamity in the Caucasus* (Carlotta Gall and Thomas de Waal, 1998).

Author's Notes

Notation

A dash (–) means that a character is interrupted. A slash (/) means that the next character to speak starts speaking at that point (what follows the slash need not be completed, it is there to indicate the character's train of thought). Ellipses (. . .) indicate that a character has interrupted him or herself.

Language

All characters speak the languages they know, whether their own or indeed English. For information, I have identified the languages and given English translations of the non-English speeches (printed in square brackets and obviously not intended to be spoken).

In this text, the non-Roman script languages are phonetically transliterated. The Kavkhaz language is in fact Bulgarian, and the Drozhdani language is largely based on Azerbaijani but contains features of other Western Turkic languages. In fact, however, neither Kavkhazia nor Drozhdania are based directly on any real country.

The transliteration is intended to render the languages in a form that will be accessible to actors, to convey the equivalent sounds of the letters, rather than their correct orthography.

Scenes

Act One

One: Santa Cruz, California, early 1989

Two: Kavkhazia, eight years later

Three: Finland, two months later

Four: The same, two days later

Five: The same, the next day

Six: Geneva, three months later

Act Two

One: Kavkhazia, two years later

Two: Eastern Mediterranean, four months later

Three: The same, the next day

Four: The same, continuous

Five: Drozhdania, two years later

Characters

JAMES NEIL, *Irish, b. 1962*
FLOSS WEATHERBY, *British, b.1950*
AL BEK, *American, b.1962*
PATTERSON DAVIS, *American, b.1958*
GINA OLSSON, *Finnish, b.1956*
TOM ROTHMAN, *American, b.1942*
NIKOLAI SHUBKIN, *Kavkhazian, b.1947*
WAITER, *Afghan origin, b.1964*
1st DROZHDAN, *20s*
KELIMA BEJTA, Drozhdani, *b.1968*
2nd DROZHDAN, *mid 30s*
JAN OLSSON-TRÄSK, *Finnish, 12*
ERIK TRÄSK, *Finnish, 45*
ROMAN LITVINYENKO, *Kavkhazian b.1960*
HASIM MAJDANI, *Drozhdani, b.1945*
1st ORDERLY, *Swiss*
2nd ORDERLY, *Swiss*
TREVELYAN, *British, 33*
EMELA, *Drozhdani, 24*
LEN, *British, 30s*
1st KAVKHAZIAN SOLDIER, *30s*
2nd KAVKHAZIAN SOLDIER, *40s*
FATHER, *47*
MOTHER, *35*
YOUNG MAN, *20*
BOY, *10*
SAILOR, *American, female*
YURI VASILEVICH PETROVIAN, *Kavkhazian President, 52*
BODYGUARD, *Kavkhazian, 20s*
ZELIM ZAGAYEV, *Drozdhani, 31*
LOU WASSERMAN, *American, 52*
ASLAN, *Drozhdani, 12*
1st PARAMILITARY, *Afghan origin, 38*
2nd PARAMILITARY, *Drozhdani, 20s*

The play is written for fourteen actors. The doubling pattern for the first production was as follows:

Al Bek/Young Man

Floss

James/2nd Drozhdan/2nd Paramilitary

Patterson/Len

Gina/Mother

Tom/Father

Nikolai/Lou

Waiter/1st Drozhdan/2nd Orderly/Trevelyan/
  Bodyguard/Zelim/lst Paramilitary

Kelima

Jan/Boy/Aslan

Erik/Yuri Vasilevich Petrovian

Roman/2nd Kavkhazian Soldier

Hasim/1st Kavkhazian Soldier

Emela/lst Orderly/Sailor

The text published here went to press while the play was still in rehearsal. Changes may have taken place before it reached its first performance.

THE PRISONER'S DILEMMA

'The question "Why?" has two quite different meanings.
One looks backward for a cause and treats our behaviour
as determined by prior events. The other looks forward
for a purpose and treats our behaviour as subject
to our free will.'

Roger Fisher and William Ury
Getting to Yes, 1981

'The way to avoid the dangers of history-poisoning
or history-addiction is to regard history not as
a heap of facts, a mountain of oppressive memories,
but as a fertile field of inquiry and interpretations,
thus using the past as building material for the future.'

Amos Oz, 1992

'Why do we kill children? Because someday
they will grow up and we will have to kill them then.'

Serb Soldier, 1992

ACT ONE

'Traditionally, the task of conflict resolution
has been seen as helping parties who perceive
their situation as zero-sum (Self's gain is other's loss)
to reperceive it as a non-zero-sum conflict (in which both
may gain or both may lose) and then to assist parties
to move in the positive-sum direction.'

Miall, Ramsbotham and Woodhouse
Contemporary Conflict Resolution, 1999

'A peace is of the nature of a conquest,
For then both parties nobly are subdued,
And neither party loser.'

Shakespeare
Henry IV Part 2

'The British Govt. agree that it is for the people
of the island of Ireland alone, by agreement between
the two parts respectively, to exercise their right
of self-determination on the basis of consent, freely
and concurrently given, North and South, to bring about
a united Ireland, if that is their wish.'

The Downing Street Declaration,
15 December 1993

'Sinn Fein has one advantage over other parties.
We've brought a camp bed. We don't share it, of course'.

Gerry Adams, April 1998

'Arafat wanted the statement to read "We recognise the
right of Israel to live in secure and recognized boundaries",
but now agreed to change the phrase "live in secure and
recognized boundaries" to "exist in peace and security".'

Jane Corbin on the Oslo negotiations

'Is the handshaking an event, or is it a gesture?'

Shimon Peres, 1993

ACT ONE

Scene One

*Early 1989. An anonymous meeting room, in an American
university. A large table, at which* JAMES NEIL, *an Irish man
in his late 20s and* FLOSS WEATHERBY, *a British woman in
her late 30s are sitting on one side, opposite* AL BEK, *a white
American man in his mid 20s,* PATTERSON DAVIS, *a black
American in his early 30s and* GINA OLSSON, *a woman of 32,
with a slight Scandinavian accent.*

AL. OK. Let's run this through again.

FLOSS. Go on.

PATTERSON. We are here to make our position absolutely
    clear to you.

FLOSS. As are we. You have read our statement of non-
    negotiable demands?

AL. Of course.

FLOSS. Comrade.

    FLOSS *nods to* JAMES, *who reads:*

JAMES. They include: an immediate end to martial law,
    withdrawal of government troops from the areas of the
    indigenous peoples, the immediate release of all / political
    prisoners –

PATTERSON. Yes, we've read the statement.

FLOSS. And recognition of the PFLO as the acknowledged
    representative / of the people –

PATTERSON. As you will know on our part that there is no
    question of a return to normal until your campaign of violence

is ceased completely. And I stop having to write letters to
the widows of policemen murdered by you terrorists.

Pause.

JAMES. I don't think we're actually asking for a return to
normal.

PATTERSON. No? I thought you wanted / an end to martial
law –

FLOSS. Not 'normal' as in the selling off of our ancestral
lands to the American imperialists. Not 'normal' as in the
vicious exploitation of the workers in the cobalt mines.
Which should be theirs by right.

JAMES (*consulting a paper*). Chromium.

FLOSS. I'm sorry?

JAMES. The mines are chromium.

AL. Well of course we have the right to sell rights to exploit
our national resources to anyone we like. We are the
government.

FLOSS. Hm!

AL *glances at* GINA, *hoping she'll come in. She doesn't, so
he carries on:*

AL. But I must tell you, that since last year's wave of strikes,
and now your threat to bomb the mines, not to mention your
campaign of taking foreign hostages, the likelihood of
investment in the mining industry is pretty limited. By
American imperialists or anybody else.

JAMES. Particularly given that United Nations resolution –

PATTERSON (*under* JAMES' *speech*). Well, you know . . .

JAMES (*simultaneous*). – of last summer declaring the
government to be illegitimate.

PATTERSON. Well, you know my attitude to UN resolutions!

FLOSS. Which it would be simplicity itself to have withdrawn.

PATTERSON. Oh how?

FLOSS. Stop arresting workers for asserting basic human rights.

JAMES. Get your soldiers off our streets.

AL. We'd be delighted to. Just as soon as you stop taking innocent civilians hostage.

JAMES. Which can happen just as soon as you release all members of the people's army.

PATTERSON. No problem. Just as soon as you declare an unconditional cessation of your terrorist campaign.

FLOSS. You say 'cessation'. I hear 'surrender'.

AL. You say 'people's army', I hear 'terrorist conspiracy'.

PATTERSON. A conspiracy they want us to legalise!

GINA *has been looking in her papers.*

GINA. In fact, they don't want to be legalised. Which would obviously involve accepting the government's authority. What they want is to be treated as the legitimate representative of the tribal peoples.

Slight pause.

In the same way as I think, although sure they want all prisoners to be released, their immediate demand is for them to be treated not as criminals but as political. Sounds pretty mild to me.

JAMES. Uh – does that help?

GINA. I merely make these points.

FLOSS. I'm sorry, aren't we going round in circles here?

A 47-year-old American professor, TOM ROTHMAN, *emerges from the audience.*

TOM. Well, you could say that we've reached an impasse.

JAMES *stretches back in his chair.*

JAMES (*mock Irish*). 'Glory be to Jayzus'.

TOM. And as everybody put their case impeccably, I wonder how that happened?

Slight pause.

AL. The bastards wouldn't budge.

FLOSS. Well, we kept to our positions in the briefing book.

JAMES. Implacably.

TOM. Yes, so you did. Has anybody seen the James Dean movie *Rebel without a Cause*?

Very slight pause.

AL. Yes, Professor, I have seen the movie.

TOM. Do you remember how it ends?

AL. Well, as I recall . . . two guys decide to drive two cars extremely fast straight at each other. And the one who swerves first loses.

TOM. In the sense of losing face. Miss Weatherby, you're driver A. Mr Davis here is Driver B. Run through your options.

FLOSS. Well, to swerve or not to, I suppose.

TOM. And if you swerve, but he drives on?

FLOSS. I lose.

TOM. And if you both swerve?

FLOSS. I still lose?

TOM. You share the loss of face. But if you drive straight on, what happens?

FLOSS. Well, he swerves, and so I win.

TOM. Or?

FLOSS. Boom.

TOM. So between, at worst, a loss of face, and – boom, what do you think you're likely to decide?

FLOSS. I'm thinking rationally?

TOM *gestures 'of course'.*

I swerve.

TOM. Mr Davis, do you agree with Miss Weatherby's analysis?

Pause.

PATTERSON. I do.

TOM. Presumably you reached the same conclusion.

PATTERSON. Yes.

TOM. And so knowing that the overwelming likelihood is that Miss Weatherby will swerve, what do you do?

PATTERSON. I do the . . . Or, I guess . . . I might consider . . .

TOM. 'Might'?

Pause.

And by the same token,

Gesture to AL.

'Hey they won't really blow the mines, let's go in and arrest the leadership'. Or the rebels think: 'Come on, they'll never bomb the villages, but just one suitcase full of semtex and goodbye downtown'. Particularly if the next best option is some kind of mutual humiliation. As you might say also, take two superpowers, and a conflict over one side's missiles on a small cigar-shaped island off the other's coastal waters, and because the choice is standing firm or losing face, you have two superpowers each trying to persuade the other they might be insane enough to stick to their position even if it ends with blowing up the world.

AL. But surely the Cuba crisis wasn't really like that.

TOM. No?

AL. No. What really happened was a perfectly reasonable compromise in which the Soviet Union removed their missiles in exchange for the US not invading Cuba. Which was what they really wanted all along.

TOM. Right. So how might we have found out what was really wanted here?

Pause.

PATTERSON. Well, we didn't ask too many questions.

TOM. No. But I was interested in Miss Weatherby's rhetorical device. 'You say . . . ceasefire?'

FLOSS. Cessation.

TOM. ' . . . but I hear surrender'. Which in that form is a kind of accusation: you claim to be asking for suspension of hostilities, but you won't be satisfied until we've given up. But if, say, Miss Olsson was drawing up a diplomatic brief for the Swedish UN delegation, she might use the same device to explore the gap between both sides' positions and their interests.

GINA. I'm sorry, I don't understand.

TOM. The difference between what the rebels say and what they really want.

GINA. What they say *is* what they want, presumably.

TOM. What, like the Russians say: 'I'm going to keep my Cuban missiles come hell or high water'. But we hear – what you really want is to protect your friend.

GINA *shrugs.*

FLOSS. I think . . . well I assume . . . what the Professor means is . . . They say they have the right to sell the mines to anyone they like, but we're actually hearing that unless the US cavalry arrives damn quickly the economy goes down the tube.

TOM. And on the other side?

AL. Well, they're saying they won't give up a square rock of their ancestral mountain, but I'm hearing what they really want is to share some of the benefits.

GINA. They would maybe like not to be exploited.

AL. Sure. As they wouldn't be if the government gave leasing rights to the Americans, with strings attached on profit share and wages and conditions and the like.

TOM. Good. And the prisoners?

JAMES. Unconditional release. (*Nod to* GINA.) In the long
term.

TOM. And the short term?

JAMES. Grant political status.

TOM. And if you were the government, what would you say?

JAMES. I'd say . . . I guess, speaking as the government,
I'd say . . . that political status wouldn't be too desperate
to concede. In exchange for what we want, which is the
hostages' release. That's 'we' the goverment and 'they' the
rebels. Obviously.

TOM (*to* GINA). While on the central issue of the talks,
I think, the most interesting point was actually yours.

GINA. Oh, yes?

TOM. That the rebels' real interest wasn't being legalised but
in being seen as legitimately speaking for the native people.
Now who else has a problem with legitimacy?

PATTERSON. Well, the government, with the United Nations.

TOM. So might there be a mechanism for both government
and rebels to make themselves legitimate before each other
and the world?

GINA. Well, you know, Professor, I would imagine that the
government might call some kind of popular election.

TOM. I'll be jiggered. So why not just announce the date right
now?

PATTERSON. Because there isn't any guarantee that the rebels
won't intimidate the population.

TOM. But surely there's no problem for the rebels. They've the
prospect of a civilian administration. The promise of free
and fair elections.

FLOSS. 'Prospect'. 'Promise'.

TOM. Yes. And of course the problem is, as soon as either side
suggests a swerve, the other side digs in.

JAMES. As is the way when driving dubious analogies towards each other at considerable speed.

TOM. Or alternatively, you might find a different game to play.

Slight pause.

Two guys arrested for a robbery. They're kept apart. Miss Weatherby is their interrogating officer. What does she do?

FLOSS. Well, what tends to happen in the movies is that you tell them both the other one is going to rat on them.

TOM. And if Mr Bek rats and Mr Neil stays silent?

JAMES. Mr Neil is jiggered.

TOM. And Mr Bek gets off scot-free. But if they both rat on the other one then it's only fair they get time off for co-operating with the police. So their choice is either staying silent and risking going down forever, or ratting for a shorter sentence if not getting off scot-free.

JAMES. I'm ratting.

AL. Ditto.

TOM. Fine.

FLOSS. But that's not the best option surely.

TOM. No.

FLOSS. Because, presumably, if they do the best thing for the other one then they do better for themselves.

JAMES. Aha.

TOM. How so?

FLOSS. Well, because, if they both rat then they get the shorter sentence. But if they both stay silent they walk free?

TOM. So the dilemma is: they have to be assured the other guy is either nice enough or smart enough to work that out.

AL. No way.

JAMES. On either count.

TOM. So it all comes down to finding someone else who you can trust.

AL. Ain't *that* the truth.

TOM. And luckily we have that man. Mr Davis, you have been appointed by the Secretary General of the United Nations to assess the situation in our country and to recommend the course of action the UN should take.

PATTERSON. I have?

TOM. You have.

PATTERSON. Clearly this man has not heard of the three great lies.

TOM. Go on.

PATTERSON. The check is in the mail, my wife doesn't understand me, I'm from the UN and I'm here to help you.

TOM. But with this necessary caveat in mind . . .

PATTERSON. Surely, the moment that the ceasefire and the date of the election are announced, we assemble an international UN force acceptable to both sides, charged with monitoring the elections and the ceasefire, and we send it in.

TOM. And both sides walk off free.

GINA. But surely all of this relies on the idea that everyone agrees on what is best.

Pause.

TOM. Go on.

GINA. That always the rational thing to want to do is stopping fighting. Even if you are the underdog, and the only way of achieving your objective is the use of force. Whereas it might be if the choice is peace or justice it is better that peace waits a while.

Slight pause.

TOM. Does anyone agree?

FLOSS. I'd put it slightly differently. I'd say . . . the assumption isn't just that when peace and justice clash, you go for peace. It's that what you dismiss as just positions, as the rhetoric and emotional indulgence that you've got to clear away to find out people's real interests, that this is actually their hopes and dreams. And that those hopes and dreams are just as fundamentally an interest as how their government is run. You see, I don't think people should be asked to sacrifice their language or their culture or their vision of the future for what you see as their immediate self-interest . . . When what you're asking them to do effectively is give up who they are.

GINA. Well, of course, this is the other side of the same coin.

FLOSS. Oh, is it?

GINA. He says: Surrender principles for peace, you turn everything into an issue of the individual. You express your 'feelings', you articulate your 'dreams', and behold the water's clean, there's universal healthcare, your kids can read and you're not living in a shanty town.

FLOSS. No, I don't think that's what I'm saying . . .

GINA. Whereas I would say that the consequence of treating these things as a game is to ignore the fact that in this world some people have much power whereas some do not. And if the powerful extend an empty hand then the last thing that the powerless should do is shake it.

FLOSS. Oh, no, I'm all for shaking hands.

GINA. And no doubt listening to the ocean, finding inner space and reaching out to touch the hand that bites you.

Slight pause. NIKOLAI SHUBKIN, *42, speaks from the audience.*

NIKOLAI. Um, might maybe I make brief point now Professor Rothman on this conversation.

TOM. Professor Shubkin. Please.

NIKOLAI. All I care to say now . . . you must please excuse my English . . .

TOM *demurs.*

. . . is this point. That now since 40 year we seem but to
have one choice – triumph of US imperialism or total
victory of worldwide working class. And so we play so
often driving car fast at each other so to see who first will
blink. Or if not all this time we sit down in our cell and fail
to work out what the other guy across jail courtyard plan to
do. But now maybe for brief moment we come out of cell
into bright ray of light at least. I say we pray we do not
miss our chance.

TOM. I should explain that Professor Shubkin is a former
member of the Institute of World Economics and
International Relations of the Soviet Academy of Sciences,
saw distinguished service in Afghanistan and is visiting
with us this semester from the University of Krum.

Pause. AL *looks surprised.*

And of course you're both right, there are limitations to
these theories. But nonetheless, they deal with something
desperately important. Because as Professor Shubkin says,
what is happening inside the Soviet Union and the Eastern
Bloc gives the peacemakers – gives us – the chance not just
to end the cold war but to confront those smaller but
persistent and intractable dilemmas which could not exist
without it. But as Miss Weatherby points out, unlike the
cold war, to resolve these conflicts we are asking people to
give up their dreams. Or at least, to change their dreams to
ones that they can share with people they've been taught to
see as less than human. To sacrifice their pasts in the
interests of a better future.

Slight pause.

Which is why we've spent this time together. And why
we've invited people like Professor Shubkin here to join us.

Pause.

I am instructed to remind all those who are leaving Santa
Cruz this evening that if they haven't yet checked out they
should do so now. And that for all parties there will be a

glass of wine to celebrate the conclusion of the seminar. Thank you and good afternoon.

The seminar breaks up. TOM *to the group:*

Well, thank you all.

Acknowledgment.

JAMES. Oh, please, don't mention it.

FLOSS. Thank *you.*

TOM *punches* PATTERSON *on the shoulder.*

TOM. Hey and Special Representative Pat *Davis.*

NIKOLAI *appears from the audience;* TOM *goes over to him.* JAMES *stands, takes out his business card and hovers.* PATTERSON *smiles, gathers his papers and goes.* GINA *puts her papers in her file.* FLOSS *opens a big notebook and makes notes about the session.*

Kolya. Thank you for your intervention.

NIKOLAI. I enjoy most greatly Mr Davis's three big lie.

JAMES. Ah well, in fact, you know / there is another –

NIKOLAI. Though in our country we have little bitty different style. One, all shops sell oranges on Monday. Two, all quota are complete on Friday. Three, come up from your cellars you have nothing to fear.

TOM. Well perhaps that too will change.

JAMES. Well, as I say / that's not the only –

TOM. Now, Kolya, you must meet Al Bek. Who's a post-graduate in international trade law here, and whose favourite saying is: There's never been a war between two countries with McDonald's.

GINA *shakes her head and goes out, catching* TOM'*s eye for a moment as he turns and goes out too.*

JAMES. Um, professor . . .

But TOM *is gone.*

AL. Hi. In fact / my folks –

NIKOLAI. How do you do.

AL. Presumably that was a set-up.

NIKOLAI. Set up?

AL. Presumably your intervention was previously planned.

Pause.

NIKOLAI. Professor Rothman most delightful man. He very much want to reassure me how all happenings here at Santa Cruz is most strict among ourselves.

AL. It's rare to meet someone from Krum.

Pause.

NIKOLAI. Well, certainly in upstate California.

In Kavkhaz:

Ot Kafkáziya li ste? [Are you Kavkhazian by origin?]

AL. I'm Kavkhazian by origin. But I don't speak the language.

NIKOLAI. Maybe you speak other language.

AL. No. My mother occasionally speaks Kavkhaz at home. And pop has got a Drozdhan joke.

NIKOLAI. So you born mix race?

AL. No. I'm single race. I was born in the Union of Soviet Socialist Republics. My mom's a half-hearted kind of Christian and my father's a lapsed Muslim. Now we're all American.

NIKOLAI. And your father's Drozhdan joke?

AL. What did Jesus tell the Kavkhars? 'Don't move till I get back'.

Slight pause.

NIKOLAI. And once again I am set up I think.

AL *smiles.*

But you also I suppose.

AL. Oh, yes?

NIKOLAI. In the James Dean movie they do not drive straight toward each other but side by side toward big cliff. But Professor Rothman version little bit much better for his game.

AL. Aha.

NIKOLAI turns to JAMES.

NIKOLAI. So sorry. I think I interrupt you.

JAMES. No.

NIKOLAI. Well, there she go.

NIKOLAI goes. AL looks round, and then goes out. FLOSS closes her notebook. JAMES is putting his business card back in his wallet.

FLOSS. Is that a business card?

JAMES. Yes. Please.

He hands her the card. That's not what she meant.

FLOSS. Oh, right. Well, after all . . .

JAMES. . . . it's what these jamborees are for.

FLOSS (*looks at the card*). So were you sent here by your University?

JAMES. No, I'm doing it on my own recognisance.

FLOSS. Why's that?

JAMES. I was informed it would look good on my CV.

FLOSS. Ah. Right.

JAMES. All terribly disreputable.

FLOSS. No . . . No, I find it rather sweet. Like when we were saying what we thought we'd be in five years' time and you were the only person to say 'diplomat'.

JAMES. You found that *sweet*?

She takes a leaflet from her file and scribbles on it, circling a telephone number.

FLOSS. So much so that I'd most appreciate it if you would call and let me know if you succeed. Or if you don't. Or if you decide that what you really want to do is something else.

GINA reenters with her suitcase, which she lays down and opens, to pack her files away.

JAMES. You're with Helping Hand.

FLOSS. And doesn't that just say it all?

JAMES. You said you were an actress.

FLOSS. Yes I did.

JAMES. Helping Hand is a international aid agency run by Quakers.

FLOSS. There are Quaker actors. And there are people who were actors who end up being something else.

JAMES (*with a nod towards* GINA). Like the scourge of Marxist fundamentalists.

FLOSS. Scourge?

JAMES. Most effectively I thought.

FLOSS. Well, it's an ancient argument.

JAMES. What is?

FLOSS. Free the streets or free your head.

JAMES. And you go for the latter.

FLOSS. I go for seeing them as complementary.

She realises JAMES *is looking at* GINA. *Standing:*

A most attractive Marxist fundamentalist.

Slight pause.

JAMES. So hence, I had assumed, attached.

FLOSS. To a husband and a child. But neither I think entirely to her satisfaction.

FLOSS *goes to* GINA *and puts her hand out.*

Well, so long.

A moment. Then GINA *shakes* FLOSS*'s hand.*

GINA. Goodbye.

FLOSS. In fact, there is a game that actors play. You get in pairs and you shake hands. Then you shut your eyes, walk backwards till you hit an obstacle, and then you move around the room, your eyes still shut, your hand outstretched, trying to find the hand you shook before. And do you know? It almost always works.

GINA. What, if you really 'listen' to the hand?

FLOSS. Well, obviously, you must believe it's possible. Otherwise, nothing works at all.

As she leaves, to JAMES*:*

I'd go for it. After all, it's what these jamborees are for.

She goes out. JAMES *and* GINA*, left a little uncomfortably alone together.*

JAMES. So, have you had a drink?

GINA. No.

JAMES. Can I get you one?

GINA. No thank you.

JAMES. You're off tonight.

GINA. 'Off'?

JAMES. Going.

GINA. So it would appear.

JAMES. To Stockholm.

GINA. Denver. But it would actually be Helsinki.

JAMES. 'Olsson'.

GINA. The capital of a country under foreign rule for 700 years.

JAMES. I'm sorry.

GINA. Good. In fact, Finland is the Swedish word. The natives call it Suomi.

JAMES. I never knew that.

GINA. It amuses us, when the world asks that we solve their problems. We're from a cold north country with a language no one understands, known universally by the name imposed on us by one imperial power and living by favour of another, and, guess what, we are here to help you.

JAMES. In fact, it isn't the UN.

GINA. What isn't the UN?

JAMES. The third great lie.

AL *enters and approaches.*

GINA. Well, I always heard it as 'the Federal Government'. So what's your version?

JAMES. Well . . .

AL. Good evening.

GINA. Evening. Well?

JAMES (*embarrassed*). Oh, well . . . maybe . . .

AL. What's happening here?

GINA. James tells a joke.

AL. Well, you know, the Irish.

JAMES. Uh, perhaps . . .

AL. Hey, man . . .

JAMES. As a married woman . . .

AL. Can this be the case?

GINA. Yes it is. How do you know?

Pause.

JAMES. You said so, when we had to introduce ourselves in three well chosen sentences.

GINA. No, I didn't. As I don't.

JAMES. Well then I . . . maybe . . . there she goes.

Flummoxed, he goes.

AL. What joke?

GINA. The third great lie. I guess the porno version.

AL. I'm not going to come in your mouth.

GINA. Precisely.

A slightly edgy pause.

AL. He was trying to make out?

GINA. Yes, I presume so.

AL. It's a funny way to go about it. After a weekend's concentrated training in the tactics of resolving seemingly intractable dilemmas.

GINA. I do not regard the two activities as comparable.

AL. Oh no? I'd say they were / absolutely –

GINA. In this I am with Mr Neil. For the last three days we have been plagued with inappropriate analogies.

AL. Oh yes?

GINA. An authoritarian dictatorship and a people's liberation movement are not in fact two criminals who have done a robbery together. They are not two young men driving cars.

AL. Nor are they resolvable by reaching out and touching British hippy actresses.

GINA *looks at* AL.

GINA. Well at least I guess she doesn't want to give the world a happy meal.

AL. So were you ever touched by feelings of compassion for the miserable and the oppressed?

GINA. Compassion's how you start, not how you stay.

AL. That's more about your anger.

GINA. Oh for heaven's sake.

AL. Because you see, if I was you I'd think there was a real space, now, to create a new kind of society, amid the wreckage of the places my folks came from. But of course to make that work you'd need to open up your mind, to take a leap into the dark, to accept that doing better means you can't do best. So that might not be of interest to you.

GINA *going to pick up her bags.*

GINA. Yes, well, I ought to . . .

AL. Hey. In fact, he oversimplified the game.

GINA. What game?

AL. The prisoner game. Both staying silent isn't actually the best, because you have to share the loot. The best is if I rat and you stay shtum and you're inside forever.

GINA. Aha. So reaching out and touching is not quite best after all.

AL. No, but it's better than the other options. And, hey, money isn't everything. And you end up walking free.

GINA. Well, I'll be jiggered.

AL. Just remind me, where d'you plan to be in five hours' time?

GINA. In five hours' time, I will be on an aeroplane to Denver.

AL. Oh, of course. Otherwise there's a risk you'd end up listening to the ocean.

A WAITER*, of Afghan origin, has entered with a tray of drinks. He hovers.*

GINA. In fact, there is an instance, much more instructive than the prisoner's dilemma. A kind of – riddle, if you like. You go into a room, and there are two unmarked doors. One door leads to a future of unbounded, wondrous possibility and the other to a bleak and miserable past. And there's two men in the room, one who always lies and one who always tells the truth. And they know which door is which, and which of them is which, and you don't. But there is one question you can ask to find out what to do.

AL. Well, you ask 'What day is it today?'

GINA. You've only got one question.

AL. Ah.

WAITER. I think you'll find you say as follows: 'If I was to ask you "What door should I go through?", what would you say?'. To which question, the truthteller answers 'That one'. And the liar answers 'That one' too. As of course, he lies about the fact he'd lie.

GINA. That's right. Thank you.

WAITER. You're welcome.

He turns to go.

AL. Hey, you could settle something else here.

WAITER. Yes?

NIKOLAI *enters as:*

AL. I have a friend who has a choice. She can take the easy option, do the thing she's planned. Or she can take a risk, for once, she can junk the plan and take a leap into the dark. So if you were me, what would you advise?

NIKOLAI. Oh, I'd say, Mr Bek, you would advise her to take the lazy way. But then I am Kavkhazian.

He takes a drink from the WAITER, *who smiles quizzically and goes out.*

This young man I discover is a mathematic student from Kabul. He come here when he realise real choice is no more communism-capitalism but the modern world or rule by mujahedeen. I wonder sometimes if that may be in our country too.

AL. I . . . hear you.

NIKOLAI. Ah. An interesting phrase. In English mouth, he mean 'Yes, I agree, but of course I cannot say'. While in America it mean, there's no need to repeat, I am rejecting what you say already. So when you say 'I hear', maybe we do not hear the same. (*To* AL.) I think she hear you in American.

He goes out. AL *turns to* GINA.

GINA. I wonder if it's true, about the touch thing.

AL. Sorry?

GINA. It's a . . . thing of Miss Floss Weatherby's. Sounds remarkably unlikely. Still. Who knows.

AL. Uh . . . do you mean . . . ?

GINA. You heard.

Scene Two

Eight years later. A church bell chimes the hour. The first floor of what appears to be a derelict house. We are in Drozhdevnya/ Drozhdania, the southern province of the former Soviet Republic of Kavkhazia.

On the floor, a car battery, electric leads, a power drill. A young DROZHDAN MAN *lies asleep on a mattress.*

Upstage, a NAKED MAN *is tied to a battered office chair on castors. He has an airport duty-free bag over his head, and a gag tied over it round his mouth. A hole has been torn in the bag for him to breathe, but he cannot see.*

As the chime completes its cycle, the trapdoor in the floor suddenly bangs open. The 1st DROZHDAN *leaps up as two people come through; a* 2nd DROZHDAN MAN *in his mid 30s and* KELIMA BEJTA, *who is 29. They are all informally dressed in cheap Western-style clothes, but wrapped up well against the cold. They speak in what they see as their national language, Drozhdani.*

2nd DROZHDAN (*Drozhdani*). Size dediyim kimi, o kishi hech tapinmas burada. [I told you, he's quite safe. No one will find him here.]

KELIMA (*Drozhdani, to* 1st DROZHDAN). Tamam, haradadir? [OK. Where is he?]

1st DROZHDAN (*Drozhdani*). Arkhadadir. [In the back.]

KELIMA (*Drozhdani, to* 1st DROZHDAN). Bir shey dedi mi? [Has he said anything?]

1st DROZHDAN (*Drozhdani, to* 2nd DROZHDAN). Sana dedikhlarimden bashqa yokh. [Only what I told you].

2nd DROZHDAN (*Drozhdani, to* 1st DROZHDAN). Yoldash, bu yoldash tugay-komutani Bejta! [Comrade, this is Comrade Brigade-leader Bejta!]

KELIMA (*Drozhdani, to* 2nd DROZHDAN). Drozhdanja danishir mi? [Does he speak Drozhdani?]

1st DROZHDAN (*Drozhdani*). Zannetmam.[Not as far as I know.]

KELIMA (*Drozhdani*). Ingilisja danishir mi? [Does he speak English?]

   1st DROZHDAN *shrugs.*

   Do you speak English?

1st DROZHDAN (*Drozdhani*). Bir az. [Just a bit.]

KELIMA. So how much is 'az'?

2nd DROZHDAN. I think enough.

   1st DROZHDAN *shrugs, acquiescing.*

KELIMA. OK. You tell him first he is in our country but he cannot speak our language and we do not speak language of occupying power. He speaks no English, is tough shit.

1st DROZHDAN. OK.

KELIMA. Second will be: you tell him that we know he spy.

1st DROZHDAN. Sure thing.

   KELIMA *realises* 1st DROZHDAN *isn't writing any of this down.* KELIMA *takes a deep breath and takes out a spiral bound notebook in which she jots down headings.*

2nd DROZHDAN (*Drozhdani*). Avvali, ziyaareti 'purposes of tourism' ichin dedi. [At first he say his visit is for 'purposes of tourism'.]

KELIMA. Oh, yuh?

1st DROZHDAN. But now 'I wish to speak to member of military council'.

KELIMA. And you tell him even so we think him Khavkhar spy and we have good right to kill him by first rule of war.

She rips off the sheet of paper and gives it to the 1st DROZHDAN. *In Drozhani:*

Gatir onu. [Go fetch him.]

1st DROZHDAN. And *you* cannot tell him this?

KELIMA. How many women please are there on military council?

The 1st DROZHDAN *goes upstage, to push the* NAKED MAN *forward on his castored chair.* KELIMA *sees the leads.*

2nd DROZHDAN (*Drozhdani*). Majlis-i Askarin durushu nadir bu kishi haqqinda? [What is the military council position on this man?]

KELIMA (*Drozhdani*). Khoshbakht deyillar. Bunlar na? [They are not happy with it. What are these?]

The 2nd DROZHDAN *smiles knowingly.*

2nd DROZHDAN. 'First rule of war'.

The 1st DROZHDAN *wheels the* NAKED MAN *forward.*

1st DROZHDAN. I speak for Comrade of Military Council! There is three things we say to you! First that as you will not speak forbidden tongue we do not speak tongue you make compulsory for us.

KELIMA *nods, graciously: the* 1st DROZHDAN *has put it rather well.* 1st DROZHDAN *leans into the man:*

1st DROZHDAN. We know how you are spy of Kavkhaz Military Intelligence – and so by rule of war we think OK we kill you. In fact, more than just OK, it is traditional.

The MAN *is squirming.*

But first we wire you up to nice car battery and bake your balls.

KELIMA can't say anything but is furious. 1st DROZHDAN
*picks up the two leads and puts them together to create a
short circuit with its ominous 'tzzzt' sound. The* MAN
shakes and quivers in desperate fear. Finally, KELIMA
*writes something on her notebook pad, tears it off and
hands it to the* 1st DROZHDAN.

1st DROZHDAN. Do you have codeword?

The MAN *nods. The* 1st DROZHDAN *doesn't know how
he's going to write it. The* 2nd DROZHDAN *hands the
paper and a pen to him.*

2nd DROZHDAN. Write him please.

The MAN *scrawls something on the pad and hands it back.*
2nd DROZHDAN *hands it to* KELIMA *who looks at it and
nods. She scribbles, tears the page off and hands it to the*
1st DROZHDAN.

1st DROZHDAN. OK we do not kill you. But no talk no
ceasefire till our prisoner are release.

2nd DROZHDAN (*Drozhdani, to* KELIMA). Bunun Majlis-i
Askarin tarafindan kaabul olajaini aminsin mi? [Are you
completely sure this will be accepted by the Military Council?]

KELIMA *nods violently as she hands over another sheet.*

1st DROZHDAN. This message please you take back now
from free Drozhdania. Please understand?

The MAN *nods.* 1st DROZDHAN *looks to* KELIMA, *who
makes the throat slitting gesture.*

OK, game over.

KELIMA *points downwards and goes down with the* 2nd
DROZHDAN.

Well, buddy, it seem we do not bake your ball together after
all.

KELIMA *comes back up, quickly. She hands a note to the*
1st DROZHDAN.

(*In some surprise.*) Chapter 10, verse 92.

He doesn't know what to do with the piece of paper.
KELIMA *takes it and puts it in the* MAN's *hands, folding them round the paper.*

2nd DROZHDAN (*in Drozhdani, from below*). Yoldash Tugay-Komutani! [Comrade Brigade Leader!]

KELIMA *goes quickly downstairs.*

1st DROZHDAN. OK. Well, buddy. You take now message home from Holy Book. In the name of God, the compassionate, the merciful.

Scene Three

Two months later. Finland. The living room of a middle-class house. The house is on the side of a hill, so the entrance is above, and people coming from outside come downstairs. There are two floor level exits: one to a playroom; the other to a dining room and, we imagine, a kitchen beyond. The interior design is almost satirically Scandinavian: clean, clear, simple, scrubbed and stripped. There is a computer and a printer set up at a table, and some battered luggage in the corner.

A 12-year-old boy, JAN, *enters on the upper level and comes downstairs. He carries a schoolbag and is listening to rock music on headphones. He sings along to a late 90s British song, loudly, in English, but without much regard to the sense of the words.*

GINA *enters from the dining room with a tray of bottles of wine and water, and nibbles in bowls.* GINA *speaks to her son in Finnish.*

GINA (*Finnish*). Jan, ne tulevat pian. [Ah Jan. They'll be here soon.]

JAN *sits down at the computer, still singing.* GINA *gets in his eyeline and waves.*

Jan, mä sanoin, että ne tulevat pian! [Jan, I said, they'll be here soon!]

JAN (*Finnish, taking the phones off*). Mitä? [What?]

GINA (*Finnish*). Minä sanoin, että vieraat tulevat pian. [I said, the guests will soon be here.]

JAN (*Finnish*). Ai jaa? [Oh, yes?]

GINA (*Finnish*). Ja me tarvitsemme tämän huoneen. [And I'm afraid I need this room.]

> JAN '*hmphs*'. GINA *goes into the adjacent dining room.* JAN *stands.*

JAN (*Finnish, calls*). Keitä ne on? [Who are they?]

GINA (*Finnish, off, calls*). Johan minä selitin. He ovat ulkomaalaisia, ja sinun pitää olla vieraanvarainen ja puhua englantia. [I've explained! They come from abroad. You will have to make them welcome with your English!]

JAN (*in English, to himself*). So I make our dear guests welcome *with my English*?

> GINA *comes back in with a tray of glasses, as* JAN *spots the suitcases.*

JAN (*Finnish*). Joko ne on täällä? [They are here already?]

GINA. Two are here already. The other two are with your father.

> *She lays out glasses and nibbles as:*

JAN. Hello, old chap. Hi there, old bean. Well, howdidoodi, pardner.

> *The front door opens upstairs and* GINA*'s husband* ERIK *enters on to the landing with suitcases.*

GINA. Well, why not. If things go sticky, you might prove a conversation piece.

JAN. What's a conversation piece?

ERIK. I think your mother means a conversation *point*.

GINA (*Finnish*). Onko kaikki kunnossa, Erik? [Erik. Is everything all right?]

ERIK (*Finnish, with a so-so gesture*). Niin ja näin. [It is all right-ish.]

ERIK *puts down the suitcases and goes back out.*

JAN. So where are both other people now?

GINA. I'm afraid they're in your playroom. In deep conversation, when I look last.

JAN. They are *where*?

GINA. I told you.

ERIK *is followed back in by* ROMAN LITVINYENKO *and* NIKOLAI SHUBKIN. ROMAN *is in his mid-30s, stylishly but casually dressed; his English is good.* NIKOLAI *is now 50, also casually dressed, though as before in a more obviously East European style.*

ERIK. We have some troubles at immigration.

GINA. I thought we booked the V.I.P. lounge.

ERIK. Yes, so did we. Unfortunately we did not have quite the right accreditation.

ERIK, NIKOLAI *and* ROMAN *are coming down the stairs into the room.*

JAN (*to his* MOTHER). In my *playroom*?

GINA. Only for three days.

NIKOLAI. And plus we are a little underdress for V.I.P.s I think. Mrs Olsson, so pleased I am to see you one more time.

ROMAN. Still too maybe.

GINA. Of course not. Professor Shubkin.

ERIK. It really wasn't anything to do / with how you're dressed –

NIKOLAI. Kolya, I hope.

GINA. Then Gina.

ROMAN. You see, we are not entirely sure / how we are supposed –

GINA. Please, everything is fine.

ERIK. So, Roman, this is –

ROMAN. Your wife. I am so very pleased to meet you. I have heard so much from Nikolai Mikhailovich. From Professor Shubkin.

GINA *puts out her hand to* ROMAN.

GINA. Gina.

ROMAN *shakes* GINA*'s hand.* ERIK *goes towards the drinks.*

ERIK. And, so . . .

JAN. Ahem.

GINA. And Jan, our son.

NIKOLAI. Well, hi there, Jan.

JAN. Well howdidoodi there old chum.

ERIK. And now, I'd guess we could all use / a drink –

GINA. Jan, your supper's in the kitchen. With the video.

NIKOLAI. Aha.

ROMAN. We see you soon again I hope.

JAN. Well, it is my house.

NIKOLAI. So long.

ROMAN. And where are – the others?

JAN (*as he goes*). They're in my playroom, in deep conversation. Ciao.

JAN *goes.*

ROMAN. And are they also members of organising committee of the European Games?

ERIK. No, one of them is here for medical reasons.

ROMAN (*to* GINA). I know nothing about sports. We are terrified that we are called upon to prove our status.

NIKOLAI. No doubt fear which grip too our friend.

ROMAN. Well depending naturally with which disease . . .

HASIM MAJDANI, 52, has entered from the playroom. He carries a briefcase and is in a suit and tie. With him is KELIMA, *dressed in severe, faintly paramilitary dark clothing. She has a briefcase also.*

HASIM. Good evening.

ROMAN. Nothing too disabling I am glad to see.

HASIM. I beg your pardon?

ERIK. Dr Majdani, who is Director of the Free Hospital at Bazarat or as you know it Basda Brod. And here for consultations on his medical responsibilities.

NIKOLAI. 'Free hospital'.

HASIM. Which is accuse I know that he is front for terrorism. In fact, I am arrest and throw in jail for being his director. But so happily I am release since two week now.

No one has allowed themselves to get close enough to handshakes to become an issue.

ROMAN. And . . .

KELIMA. I am Kelima Bejta and I am member of the political committee of Drozhdan Khalq Jabhasi.

ERIK. Drozhdan People's Front.

ROMAN. Of course.

NIKOLAI. And so what cover do our kind host find / for you?

ROMAN *stops him with a gesture, as* HASIM *interrupts.*

HASIM. And now please we are told who you may be.

ROMAN. I am Roman Litvinyenko. I am editor of Rámka. Which I guess translate as 'Frame'. And Professor Shubkin is deputy head of the Institute of Kavkhazian Military History at University of Krum.

KELIMA. Professor or maybe General Shubkin.

NIKOLAI. Certainly not General.

GINA. But it's fair to say they are both here with the knowledge and blessing of the government in Krum. As are you with the knowledge and the blessing of the DPF.

HASIM. Well, knowledge, certainly.

ROMAN. We are here to resolve unrest in Drozhdevnya, province of former Soviet Republic of Kavkhazia.

KELIMA. We are here to discuss legitimate demand of Drozhdan people for self determination.

ERIK (*gesturing to drinks*). So, would you care to . . .

ROMAN. Thank you. I would very much like a glass of wine.

Partly in order to move, ROMAN *goes over to get his drink from* ERIK, *followed by* NIKOLAI.

NIKOLAI. Me also.

ERIK. Please help yourselves. Miss Bejta?

KELIMA. Do you have orange juice?

ERIK. Of course. Dr Majdani?

HASIM. I will have mineral water.

ERIK. Fine.

ROMAN *is helping himself at this moment, and so can pour orange juice for* KELIMA *and water for* HASIM.

HASIM. Thank you.

ERIK (*making to go*). And now, if you'll forgive me, I must attend to / making supper –

HASIM. Or if you forgive us, Mr Trask, what we must do is to discuss all ground rule of our conversation here.

ERIK. In fact / this should be –

KELIMA. In particularly your own role in this as 'facilitator'.

GINA. In fact, this is not the role of Mr Trask.

ROMAN. Oh, I had understood –

GINA. If anybody's it is mine.

Pause.

HASIM. Well, then, Mrs Trask –

ERIK. And in fact my wife's name is Gina Olsson. Although it couldn't matter less.

GINA *raises the slightest of eyebrows, and goes and gets herself a drink.*

GINA. My husband is a senior official with the Finland Ministry of Sports, who was approached by a – concerned Drozhdani person at the Kavkhazian Olympic Trials. With the suggestion that the time might be ripe for resolution of the conflict between the two parts of Kavkhazia.

ERIK. While, happily, my wife met Professor Shubkin at the University of California some years ago. And is now deputy first secretary of the Southern European Section of our Foreign Ministry.

GINA. Although – of course – it couldn't matter less.

Pause.

NIKOLAI. So it agree we do not issue invitation to 'Drozhdan People Front'?

GINA. No, as I say, it came from a concerned Drozhdani. I think a businessman, I think somehow in the nickel trade. Which I pass on to Professor Shubkin, who pass it on to the Kavkhaz government. And via a naturally long and winding road of messages we end up here.

ERIK. So might we all sit down?

ROMAN. Agreed.

He and NIKOLAI *sit.* HASIM *and* KELIMA *are consulting each other.*

HASIM. We agree also. But first it is most traditional among all Drozhdani people to present to hostess gift.

He takes a wrapped present from his briefcase and hands it to GINA. GINA *sits and opens the present a little*

*nervously. It's a lump of metal, crudely fashioned into a
bowl shape.*

It is ashtray, made from turret of water-cannon captured from
occupying force by resisting freedom fighters following
Massacre of Innocent at Bridge of Bazarat, of 22 November,
1990.

He sits, followed by KELIMA.

GINA. Thank you.

ROMAN. There is of course no section of that sentence we do
not contest.

NIKOLAI. Except maybe for 'it's an ashtray'.

GINA *puts down the ashtray.*

HASIM. But maybe you don't smoke.

GINA. Well no. But, thank you.

Slight pause.

In fact, the events of November 1990 might be a good place
to begin.

ERIK *is not sure about this.*

ROMAN. What do you mean?

GINA. I mean that sometimes it is good to start with something
on which there are differences of opinion. Of course you
have sharply different views of what happened on that day.
But it is often useful nonetheless to describe your feelings
when you heard about this, and indeed your feelings now.

Pause.

ROMAN. Miss Olsson, you are aware what happened at the
bridge of Basda Brod?

GINA. Yes, of course I am.

Pause.

ERIK. First however we should start with everybody saying
who they are, and what they expect and hope for from this
meeting.

Pause.

ROMAN. Um . . .

GINA. And then it can be helpful too for each person to present their position to the others, say for five minutes, and then for someone else to summarise what they see as the fundamentals of the other person's case.

NIKOLAI. You mean, 'You say, I hear'.

GINA. Yes, if you like.

NIKOLAI. You change your tune.

GINA. Events in Berlin, Prague and Moscow change my tune.

KELIMA. No I'm sorry this is quite ridiculous.

Slight pause.

GINA. In what way?

KELIMA. We know what mean to 'tell each other what we want and hope and feel'. It mean all problems will be solve by people get to know each other better. Being nice and upfront, 'reach out I'll be there'.

GINA. No, actually / in fact –

KELIMA. So you clear away all 'rhetoric' and 'prejudice' and find we are so much in common – bouf we are all Scandinavians.

GINA. No of course that isn't what I'm saying.

KELIMA. No? But it is quite clearly what I hear.

Difficult pause. ERIK *glances at his watch then gestures to* GINA.

GINA. Please excuse us for a moment.

She and ERIK *go out.* NIKOLAI *takes out his cigarettes.*

HASIM. What means 'you change your tune'?

NIKOLAI. And she say. We meet since eight years in California.

Reenter GINA.

GINA. My husband apologises. He has had to go off to the kitchen. If our government is not to be accused of solving pressing international problems by a policy of deliberate starvation of its politicians.

A little helpful laughter. To KELIMA *then everyone:*

Look. I am sure that if we – if this thing is going to work it must be through an understanding of the way the world looks from the other side. As the events at – Bazarat or Basda Brod – make clear, there are two histories in contest, and I suspect we need to work out how those narratives collide. All we know is that there are two large populations sharing one small place who see themselves as having separate pasts but will have to share a common future. But the most important thing is that these are your meetings and you must run them as you wish. Maybe you have your own thoughts how we might begin.

She sits.

KELIMA. We have a document.

GINA. Good. Please.

HASIM *takes out a document from his briefcase.*

HASIM. It is naturally in our language.

NIKOLAI. I fear I am not speaking Gezhekh language.

KELIMA. This document is not in 'Gezhekh language'. It is in Drozdhani language.

NIKOLAI. No more I guess than Mrs Olsson.

ROMAN. Oh I can probably translate.

This is a bit of a surprise.

I was born and brought up in Fiore.

KELIMA (*quietly*). Sukhidat.

HASIM *begins.*

HASIM (*Drozhdani*). Bu ifaada, yirminji iyun tarikhinda Drozhdan Khalq Jabhasinin Siyaasi Komitesi tarafindan muvaafaqat edildi.[The Political Committee of the Drozhdan People's Front agreed the following statement on the 20th of June.]

ROMAN. This was agreed by Political Committee of DPF 20 of June.

HASIM (*Drozhdani*). Komite, bu prinsiplarin esaasi va danishilmas olduunu sayir. [The Committee regards these principles as fundamental and non-negotiable.]

ROMAN. The Committee view principles as basic and inviolable.

HASIM (*Drozhdani*). Birinji, Har ishghalchi quvvalarin, Drozhdan torpaqtan geri chakmasiyla, Drozhdan khalqa ishlatilan butun zaraarlarin sakhlamasi. [First, the withdrawal of all occupying forces from Drozdhani soil and an end to all repressive action against the Drozdhani people.]

ROMAN. First, withdrawal of our forces from – Drozhdani soil . . . end of repressive action against Drozhdani population.

HASIM. In fact it is 'occupying force'.

NIKOLAI (*taking out a cigarette*). Beg pardon, is plan for you to read out all / this document?

HASIM. And 'Drozhdan people'.

NIKOLAI. Oh, of course.

NIKOLAI *goes and gets the ashtray.*

HASIM (*Drozhdani*). Ikinji, Drozhdan Khalq Jabhasinin, Drozhdan Khalqin / tamsilchisi olmasini, Kavkhar ishghalchilar tarafindan taninmasi – [Second, recognition by Kavkhar occupiers of the Drozhdan People's Front / as the representative of the Drozdhani people –]

NIKOLAI. Forgive me. This appear it is our only ashtray. As English it is our only common language.

He lights up. KELIMA *takes the document from* HASIM.

KELIMA (*translating the document as she goes*), Number two demand. Immediate recognising of Kavkhar occupier DKJ that is DPF in English as representative of Drozdhani people in struggle for self-determination. Third is accepting of all blame? maybe, responsibility, by occupiers for massacre of innocent at Bridge of Bazarat and for bringing of responsible for crime to justice. Four please full reparation for historic wrong performed to Drozhdan people who are forcibly deport to Khazakhstan by Stalin for so-called collaboration with invaders in Great Patriotic War. Five free all political prisoner held by occupier in concentration camp. Or no I'm sorry it 'releasing . . . '

She doesn't know the English word, so shows the paper to ROMAN.

ROMAN. Unconditionally. But as there is no concentration camp in Kavkhazia, this demand I think we may accept.

KELIMA *snorts.*

And while on the topic of objective fact, there is no 'occupying force' repressing anyone in Drozhdevnya. What exist there is a representative assembly, which the DPF refuse to recognise, which control with other thing our police. Insofar as they are consisting of those resident in Drozhdevnya, 'Drozhdani people' hold quite wide variety of religious and cultural traditions, back through many generations, no surprise because of many sites of Christianity which is religion of Kavkhazian majority, who are not of course responsible for deportations of Stalin time which is responsibility of Soviet government in Moscow. And when you say Drozhdan People's Front claim mere right to self-determination I hear secession brought about by terror, and joining up with another country namely Gezhekhstan. And what you call 'innocents' at Bazarat I understand as rioter at town of Basda Brod who try to stop a legal march in commemoration of our national heritage and which turns into a pogrom of Drozhdnevnyan Christians if Ministry of Interior does not intervene.

KELIMA. Mr Litvinyenko, I have sister die in what you say riot I hear pogrom. She is fifteen and she is sitting down on bridge and she is truncheon by your police and she fall to raging river underneath and she is drown. Like 37 other person. Sorry other rioters. So sorry actually children.

ROMAN. Miss Bejta, we have all suffered in this conflict. To suffer is not a privilege of just one side. In that, no one side has monopoly.

KELIMA. Oh, what? *You* suffer?

ROMAN. Oh, yes.

GINA. Now, this getting nowhere / we should stop this now –

KELIMA. What, you *yourself*?

JAN enters from the dining room.

JAN. Excuse me, gentlemen and ladies. My pa requests the mindless terrorists and their hatchet-faced oppressors to come in to dinner.

There is a moment of uncertainty. JAN looks to his MOTHER, then back to the others.

Oh and he ask me to inform you of house rule. No business talking over dinner. Light general conversation only. That is, if you'd be so kind.

Slight pause.

GINA. You said – you said two things. One was: The police are responsible to the representative assembly which you'd like the Drozdhan people to recognise. The second is, Dr Majdani said that he wished the DPF to be recognised as representing the Drozhdani-speaking population.

Slight pause.

I wonder, after dinner, if it would be interesting to make a simple list of what you see as the actual interests of those you represent. And see how many words turn up on both.

Slight pause. HASIM stands.

HASIM. Well, it must be a simple list. If it is in my English.

NIKOLAI *stands.*

NIKOLAI. I find it hard to think what I may tell my wife. As first thought I think I say I have dirty weekend with my secretary. But I know that she will say: Don't give me all

that shit, you can't fool me. You're off in Scandinavia
negotiating peace agreement with DPF.

NIKOLAI, HASIM *and* ROMAN *follow* JAN *into dinner.*
GINA *stops* KELIMA.

GINA. I'm sorry. I got off on the wrong foot.

KELIMA. 'Wrong foot'?

GINA. Of course you're right, about 'reach out I'll be there'.

KELIMA *looks at* GINA.

KELIMA. You know this so-call 'representative assembly' in
boycott by majority?

GINA. I do.

KELIMA. As all Drozhdan 'representative' are force to pass
Kavkhazi language test and swearing oath of loyalty to
Kavkhaz state?

GINA. Yes, so I gather.

KELIMA. Good. And maybe you will gather also that
Sukhidat main soccer team is not permitted to wear
Drozdhan national colour? Before of course team ethnic
cleanse? As ditto all state-run office, hospital and school?

GINA. Well, I didn't know about the football team.

KELIMA *makes to go.*

KELIMA. OK.

GINA. It must be difficult for you.

KELIMA (*obviously*). How so?

GINA. I understand there was a battle on the military council.
Some of your comrades felt there was no possibility of find-
ing common ground, between you and the ethnic Kavkhars.
I gather it was a close-fought thing. But you won through.

KELIMA. You know if this thing fail, then we say we are
never here.

She goes into dinner. A moment, then GINA *follows.*

Scene Four

Two days later. There is considerable evidence of last night's discussions – empty bottles, dirty glasses and crockery, full ashtrays. NIKOLAI *is still in pyjamas and a dressing gown, sitting at the computer typing in a document from a manuscript.* JAN *too is in his night things, watching over his shoulder.*

JAN. What are you doing?

NIKOLAI. I type up document.

Pause.

JAN. What's it about?

NIKOLAI. It is called Draft Declaration of Shared Principles.

Pause.

JAN. So why is it in English? Why not in your language?

NIKOLAI. We have two languages. And nobody from their side learn our language and no one from our side learn theirs.

JAN. You know, if my writing was as bad as that, I'd be sent off home to do it all again.

NIKOLAI *laughs. He leans back, lights a cigarette.*

NIKOLAI. In fact, this is not my writing. It is the Drozhdan man.

JAN. So why can't he type it out himself?

NIKOLAI. Well, you know when Jesus down on earth what he tell to Drozhdhan.

JAN. No, what?

NIKOLAI. 'Don't move till I get back'.

A moment, then JAN *gets it and laughs.*

NIKOLAI. So what d'you know about Kavkhazia?

JAN. Well, it's a country of eight million people, nestling in the shadow of – Berushka mountains, main industries heavy manufacturing and agriculture, main resources low-grade nickel and brown coal.

NIKOLAI. Nickel not so low grade.

JAN. Well, Encarta.

NIKOLAI *questions.*

Microsoft.

NIKOLAI. So, do you know of Russian doll, with smaller inside bigger?

JAN. Surely do.

NIKOLAI. Well, biggest doll is former Soviet Union. Inside for many years is Republic of Kavkhazia. Now Kavkhazia is proper country too, but inside him is largely Muslim province called Drozhdevnya which is where big mines are but which think, hey, we may be proper country also. Unfortunately, in Drozhdevnya is Kavkhazian minority of maybe third who do not think is quite such fabulous idea. And so by open up big doll all little doll blow open too.

JAN. And you all come here to sort this out?

NIKOLAI. We all come here to sort this out.

He taps the document. GINA *is coming down the stairs with shopping bags.*

JAN. And so, the future of your country is depending *on my mother?*

NIKOLAI. Sure.

JAN. Well, bloody hell.

GINA. 'Dependent' on your mother. Well, it's good to know one's son has trust.

She sees JAN*'s still in night things.*

Even if he's not yet dressed at eleven in the morning.

JAN *looks over to* NIKOLAI, *also in his nightwear, who stands, looking a little sheepish.*

Well, Professor Shubkin is at important work.

She begins to collect glasses.

NIKOLAI. I'm sorry, um . . .

GINA. No, please. You must feel free –

NIKOLAI (*gesturing at the glasses*). I meant . . .

GINA. Well, ditto. Is Roman up?

NIKOLAI. I think he is maybe back in kitchen making breakfast.

To JAN*:*

We are very late last night. Except for Miss Bejta. Who is sensible and goes to bed.

GINA. Dr Majdani?

NIKOLAI. Well, I think he still . . .

Sleeping gesture.

JAN. Well, you know what Jesus told the Drozhdans.

GINA. Sorry?

JAN. 'Don't move till I get back'.

GINA *looks fiercely at* JAN.

It's his joke.

A moment.

GINA. Good.

GINA *takes her shopping out. There is a moment of solidarity between the two under-dressed men.*

JAN. I thought it was quite funny.

NIKOLAI. Hey. You know I say the Drozhdans – well, some Drozhdans – want to be part of next door Muslim country.

JAN. Gekhestan.

NIKOLAI. Gezekhstan. Who major product is root vegetable.

JAN. I see.

NIKOLAI. And the joke is: Why do Arabs get all oil and the Gezhekhs get all turnips? And the answer is – the Gezhekhs got first pick.

JAN laughs, then stops.

JAN. Don't get it.

NIKOLAI. Well the point / maybe is that they are bit –

GINA enters, a little flustered, from the dining room.

GINA. He's praying.

NIKOLAI. Who?

GINA. Dr Majdani. I was just, um, tidying . . . and then I saw him kneeling head down on the floor.

NIKOLAI. You know, he says he is not so religious . . .

HASIM enters from the dining room, looking round.

HASIM. Good morning.

GINA. Morning.

HASIM. Forgive me, I have lost a . . . ah.

He picks up a pen, which NIKOLAI has been using, from by the computer.

NIKOLAI. Oh, I'm sorry – uh, I must have . . .

HASIM. No matter. It is only sentimental value. It is given me by President Gaddhafi. So where is Mr Litvinyenko?

GINA. We think he's in the kitchen.

HASIM. And Draft Declaration?

JAN. It's in the PC.

Slight pause.

HASIM. Well, we must hope we get it out again.

He goes out into the playroom. JAN makes to go. NIKOLAI doesn't know how to print the document.

NIKOLAI. Um . . .

JAN *picks up* NIKOLAI*'s tone and turns back.*

JAN. You want it printing out?

NIKOLAI. Yes, please. Five copy.

With aplomb, JAN *sets the printer to print, bashes the
button and watches the first sheet curl out of the printer.*

JAN. Hey. Kavkhazia: 'Pandora's Doll'.

NIKOLAI (*pleased*). Pandora's Doll.

GINA. What's this?

JAN. Well, *I'm* going to get dressed. It is eleven in the
morning.

He goes upstairs.

GINA. You know, he's got a rather – delicate, dry sense of
humour.

NIKOLAI. Your son?

GINA. Well, yes. But I was thinking of –

NIKOLAI. Colonel Gaddhafi.

GINA. Hm.

NIKOLAI. A medical professor. As you say, good sense of
humour. Quite easy sometime maybe to forget.

GINA. To forget?

NIKOLAI. On 22 November, in riot, after bridge is clear, our
police see children running downstairs to cellar. They chase
after, and find cellar floor covering in film which look like
greasy water. With big door at other end, where last boy
stand there, waiting, till police all safe inside, then toss
match on to petrol. Boy no older maybe than your son. So
when you say alternative to peace is tearing us apart, I say,
maybe this happens now already.

GINA. Would the Drozhdanis see it like that?

NIKOLAI. Let me tell you how I see it. In mid-ages yes we
are occupy by Ottoman. In modern era we are occupy by

Russia then by Soviet Union. Under Stalin many churches in Agari region smash up and even under Brezhnev period Soviet army use cave monastery for target practice. So now at least we get to own our country for first time. For us, Drozhdevnya our Jerusalem. Do we hand it back to Turk?

GINA. Yes, I remember you said something similar at Santa Cruz.

NIKOLAI. I am speaking to young Kavkhar boy I think. I do not recall you hear me.

GINA. Oh, yes. I hear you.

NIKOLAI. Aha. It all come back to me.

KELIMA *and* ERIK *have entered above. They come down the stairs.*

KELIMA. Good morning.

GINA. Morning.

ERIK. We've been walking.

KELIMA. How do you say, healthy powers?

GINA. Therapeutic.

KELIMA. Therapeutic powers of countryside.

GINA. I'm glad. I'll tell the others you're back.

To ERIK:

Dr Majdani's in the playroom.

She goes out. ERIK *goes into the playroom.* KELIMA *and* NIKOLAI *nod at each other.* KELIMA *goes to the computer and looks at the hand-corrected version of the document.*

KELIMA. This is new version of shared principles?

NIKOLAI. Yes.

KELIMA (*picks up a sheet*). Revisions from last night.

NIKOLAI. Cosmetic changes merely.

Enter GINA *and* ROMAN *from the dining room,* HASIM *and* ERIK *from the playroom.*

ROMAN. Good morning.

KELIMA (*Drozhdani*). Ah Hasim, bu na? [Ah, Hasim. What is this?]

ROMAN. Is there a problem?

KELIMA *looks to* ROMAN, *then to* HASIM:

KELIMA (*Drozhdani*). Bir problem var. [There is a problem.]

HASIM (*Drozhdani*). Na var? [What's the matter?]

The following three speeches together with the subsequent two speeches.

KELIMA (*Drozhdani*). San onlari matni dayishtirttin, khalq khalqlara, sechkilar qurallari, dil mesalasi. [You have let them change the text – people to peoples, election rules, language question.]

HASIM (*Drozhdani*). Bunlar yuzeysal . . . [These are cosmetic . . .]

KELIMA (*Drozhdani*). Yoldash Hasim, bu dayishtirmalar yuzeysal deyillar! [Comrade Hasim, these are not cosmetic changes!]

Simultaneous with:

ROMAN (*to* NIKOLAI, *in Kavkhaz*). Kakvó stáva took? [What's going on?]

NIKOLAI (*Kavkhaz*). Nyamám ponyátie. [I've no idea].

ERIK*'s looking at the printout.*

ERIK (*a little offhand*). Um, English, please. Is this – is the italic what you've not agreed?

ROMAN (*looking*). No, the italic is what we have agreed.

ERIK. Some way to go.

ERIK, ROMAN *and* NIKOLAI *turn to* HASIM *and* KELIMA.

HASIM. Yes, I am sorry. With maybe . . .

ROMAN. Yes?

HASIM. One or two so small amendments also.

Pause.

ROMAN. Hasim, we stay up to four a.m. on this.

NIKOLAI. We are here three days. We are book to leave tomorrow.

KELIMA. I have no doubt that booking may be change.

Hiatus. ERIK *decides to try and break it.*

ERIK. Call me when you'd like lunch.

ERIK *is going, as the phone rings. Although* GINA *instinctively moves to answer it,* ROMAN *gets there first.*

ROMAN (*Kavkhaz*). Álo? Izvinyávaite, gréshka. [Hallo? Ah. Sorry.]

Hands the phone to GINA.

GINA (*takes the phone*). Hallo.

In French:

Je vais bien. Mais, comment vas tu? Oui, en effet, ce n'est pas le bon moment. [Just fine. But how are *you*? Yes, in fact, this is a bad moment.]

Pause. ERIK *goes out.*

Je suis désolée, je n'en sais rien. Ce soir peut-être. À bientôt. [I'm afraid I don't quite know. Tonight maybe. 'Bye.]

She puts down the phone.

KELIMA. Do you expect a call?

GINA. No, I . . .

KELIMA. I'm sorry, I mean Mr Litvinyenko.

Slight pause. NIKOLAI *is looking quizzically at* GINA, *wondering about her call.*

ROMAN. Yes. I am waiting for a call from Krum.

HASIM. Oh, yes?

ROMAN. There is something I ask them to consider.

HASIM. I think that we agree / we make no calls –

ROMAN. On what subjects are these 'small amendments'?

HASIM. We must insist on 'peoples' not 'people' of Drozhdania.

ROMAN. I see.

KELIMA. Nor can we accept election under international observation. It must be international scrutiny.

NIKOLAI. This is small amendment?

KELIMA. And it is not right of children to be taught their Drozdhan language. But *by* Drozhdani language.

GINA. As the medium of instruction.

KELIMA. As is not I think 'cosmetic change'.

ROMAN. No indeed not. So we must discuss it.

NIKOLAI. This is everything we amend last night.

ROMAN. But there is one thing we do not amend. We agree we finish by tomorrow morning. I do not make plans to change my flight.

KELIMA. We'll work in playroom. It's easier to spread out papers.

ROMAN *looks to* GINA.

GINA. Yes of course.

HASIM, KELIMA, ROMAN *and* NIKOLAI *go out with their documents.* GINA *goes to the phone. She is picking it up when* JAN *comes downstairs, dressed. She puts it down.*

GINA (*Finnish*). Hei, kulta. [Hallo, darling.]

JAN (*Finnish*). Missä ne ovat? [Where are they?]

Enter ERIK.

GINA (*Finnish*). Pelihuoneessa. [In the playroom.]

ERIK (*Finnish*). He ovat vielä pelihuoneessa? [They're in the playroom?]

Enter ROMAN, *as:*

GINA. Mitä Kelima kertoi sinulle, kun kävitte kävelyllä?
Kertoiko hän esimerkiksi, miksi he esittävät 'hard cop soft
cop' mutta väärin päin? [So what did Kelima tell you on the
walk? Did she talk about why they're playing 'hard cop soft
cop' the wrong way round?]

ROMAN (*wryly*). English, please.

GINA. Sorry.

ROMAN. Do you have an English dictionary?

GINA. What, English-English?

ROMAN. Preferably.

JAN. Yes, I've got one. Granma Olsson gave it me for
Christmas.

GINA. Could you get it please.

JAN *goes out.*

ROMAN. Do carry on.

ERIK *and* GINA *glance at each other.*

Unless you were having light general conversation under
dinner table rule. But I think not.

GINA. Oh why not?

ROMAN. You were far too animated.

ERIK. No, we were talking about Kelima Bejta.

Slight pause.

ROMAN. And maybe how very strange that she is on faction
of military council who support these talk, but here she
plays 'hard cop'. Whereas Majdani, who is sent here clearly
as her minder, appears to give up most.

GINA. Yes that did surprise us.

ROMAN. Did she say anything about it on your walk?

ERIK. I . . . don't think I could say.

GINA. So how do you know?

ROMAN. How do I know what?

GINA. What goes on in the Military Council?

Slight pause.

ROMAN. I guess it is like Richard Nixon. Only he could open up to China. Only most militant Drozdhani can sell this deal.

JAN *has reentered.*

GINA. If deal there is.

JAN. Here's the dictionary.

ROMAN. Thank you.

JAN. Are you near a breakthrough?

GINA. No.

JAN. I am very eager not to miss it.

ROMAN. So are we.

JAN *grins and goes out.*

In fact, the situation is deceptive.

ERIK. Oh?

ROMAN. You're right of course. You make list, all kind of things come clear. Both sides want guarantees against discrimination by the other. We are loyal to majority Kavkhazian, they to majority Drozdhanian. We are both loyal to the principle of equal democratic rights for all.

GINA. That's very elegant.

ROMAN. Now we try and do the same for language issue and for Basda Brod.

GINA (*nodding to the dictionary*). What are you looking for?

ROMAN. We need a word a little short of 'friendship'.

ERIK. 'Cordial relations'.

ROMAN. The condition you are with when you are cordial related.

GINA. 'Amity'.

ROMAN. 'Amity' is good.

To GINA:

Big tip. I think she thinks you think that you can weaken her. On grounds of woman solidarity. For you she seem like western feminist, because she is angry with how men behave. But in fact she thinks concerns of western feminists are essentially trivial. A luxury, set against real problems of the world.

He goes out. ERIK *looks at the telephone, looks at* GINA.

GINA. So now he tells me.

Scene Five

The next day. In fact, early the following morning. Luggage in the corner. ROMAN, HASIM, KELIMA *and* NIKOLAI. ROMAN *is reading out a draft.*

ROMAN. OK. Recognising both their historical affinities and distinct traditions and allegiances, the parties declare their loyalty to the principle of a multi-ethnic, democratic future for the peoples of the Bela River basin. Accordingly, the Kavkhaz Government recognises the Drozhdan People's Front / as the legitimate –

NIKOLAI. Which we change to 'acknowledge'.

HASIM (*Drozhdani*). Oyle mi? [Did they?]

KELIMA (*Drozhdani*). Oyle, yadda sakhlarin mi? [Yes, you remember?] It is in exchange for word 'legitimate'.

Enter GINA *with a tray of food and drink.*

ROMAN. . . . so, 'acknowledges' the DPF as the legitimate representative of a substantial section of the population of

the province. It agrees to the setting up of a Commission of
Amity to investigate and to report on past acts of violence,
intimidation and harassment, by all parties, particularly the
events of / late November –

NIKOLAI. Particularly but not exclusively . . .

ROMAN. . . . the events of late November 1990 on the bridge
connecting Bazarat with Basda Brod. While for its part the
DPF dot-dot-dot-dots the use of violence in pursuit of its
political ambitions.

Slight pause.

NIKOLAI. And so here we are once more.

HASIM. It cannot be 'renounce'.

NIKOLAI (*wearily*). Why not?

KELIMA. Because 'renounce' make all invalid our armed
struggle.

NIKOLAI. Why?

HASIM. 'Renounce' mean it was wrong. You renounce drug-
taking or adultery.

NIKOLAI. But without you will accept the Kavkhaz
sovereignty, there is no guarantee without renouncing you
do not take up arms again.

HASIM. It cannot be.

ROMAN. It must be. I am told it must be so by Krum.

Pause.

KELIMA. This is your call.

ROMAN. Correct.

KELIMA. We agree we do not make consultation.

ROMAN. We agree that we seek agreement that will fly. I tell
you that this will not fly. You tell me it's your bottom line
and I think it's good we know your bottom line won't fly.

KELIMA. And this from horse's mouth of / your beloved
President –

ROMAN. I speak to chief of staff of President Petrovian. In fact, I speak twice. I call him back. It must be 'renounce violence'.

Enter ERIK, *with more food. He looks at* GINA *questioningly. She mouths 'renounce'.*

KELIMA. This does not happen.

ROMAN. And it cannot be declaring 'resistance' to terror, how can you resist something you are doing?

HASIM. But if we are 'terrorists' / then how can –

ROMAN. It must be 'renounce'. Implying –

HASIM. We know what it implies.

Pause.

GINA. Could it not . . . have you explored 'both sides'. Or 'all sides'. Or 'all citizens'.

ROMAN. Gina, one side is the state. How can it be 'both sides'.

KELIMA. This is impossible. I'm so sorry.

Pause.

GINA. All I'm saying is, there might be room / for some adjustment –

ROMAN. No there is no room. We accept 'ceasefire' not 'cessation'.

NIKOLAI. 'Complementary' not 'precondition'.

ROMAN. It is – it has no practical effect. It is a form of words.

KELIMA. Oh sure yes. We tell those women whose sons and husbands die for free Drozhdania we renounce them but OK because just form of words.

HASIM. I say again. So sorry. It may not be unilateral renounce.

Pause.

ROMAN. Then I'm so sorry also. We have run into the sand.

Pause.

KELIMA. This is revenge for our small amendments.

ROMAN. No. Oh no.

KELIMA. This is because we add one 's' to one word.

ROMAN. No it is not.

KELIMA. This is because we want our children to be brought up speaking their own language.

ROMAN. No. But I must say – ?

KELIMA. Yes? Yes? What must you say?

GINA (*sensing what this is provoking*). Um, Roman . . .

ROMAN. No, I must say this. This happen for two days. We take one step, they take one step, then they demand we take one more step just as they jump two step back.

KELIMA. We are here for principle negotiation. Not class for dancing.

ROMAN (*furious*). No, it is not dancing class. It is the method of the rug market. It is the tactic of the souk.

This is the worst thing to say.

It is you who are aggressors. It is you who must renounce your violence if you must gain what we are offering today. How might it any way be otherwise?

HASIM *stands, goes and picks up* KELIMA*'s luggage.*

HASIM. I think we must leave to catch our plane after three hour. There is no point now to go to bed.

KELIMA. They are never serious.

HASIM. We wait upstair.

KELIMA. I fetch my overnight thing.

KELIMA *goes into the playroom as* HASIM *heads for the stairs.* JAN *appears in a dressing gown and pyjamas.*

ROMAN (*to* GINA). You see.

HASIM. This is very obvious planned provocation.

GINA. Please, Hasim. Please.

ROMAN. You see, to find something common . . .

NIKOLAI. This is absurd.

ROMAN. It is necessary first to be . . .

HASIM (*bumping into* JAN). Ah. Hallo.

GINA. Jan. What?

JAN. I need a glass of water.

ROMAN. I'm so sorry. Do we wake you?

JAN. No. What's happening? Are people going home? Have I missed the breakthrough?

KELIMA enters with her overnight bag.

GINA. No, you haven't missed the breakthrough.

ROMAN. You see, to find something common it is needed first to be something there to find.

KELIMA. Which since noted date in 1990 it so hard to do today.

NIKOLAI. Well we can say today will not be noted date for anything.

Pause.

KELIMA. I'm hungry. I wait here.

She comes down and takes a chocolate, offering the plate to JAN.

JAN (*taking chocolate*). Thanks.

KELIMA. Maybe time now for dinner speaking rule and 'light general conversation'.

HASIM comes down and sits. Silence.

ERIK. I've a question, I've been waiting days to ask. Does anyone – did anybody realise that the 22 November is the date of John F. Kennedy's assassination?

They look at him, taken aback.

I ask because, here in the west, anyone who was alive then is supposed to remember where they were when they heard the news. I am 13 and as it happens I am dressed up in a ballgown and a long blonde wig as I am a Princess in a boys' school play.

Slight pause.

JAN. You mean like Mr Gorbachev.

NIKOLAI. Like Gorbachev?

ERIK. We became a little conscious even more about the dates of things when Jan is born in March 1985. It is the day that Mr Gorbachev is elected leader of USSR.

GINA. My 13th birthday on the other hand is the day of landing on the moon. I remember, nobody that day is very interested in my party.

Slight pause.

'One giant leap for mankind'.

Pause.

Jan, go and get your water.

JAN goes out. Silence. GINA, suddenly tempted, reaches for a cigarette. She changes her mind. She takes a chocolate instead. Finally it's NIKOLAI who can't bear it.

NIKOLAI. As it happen, I am in Dallas on that day.

GINA. For the assassination?

NIKOLAI. Great rewrite of history. No, at time of . . . Bridge, riot or whatever. It is commemorative conference on historiography of cold war. What will happen maybe if Lee Harvey Oswald miss.

ERIK. Sounds interesting.

NIKOLAI. Not so much – to me – as news come in from Basda Brod. But there is one good joke.The Moderator say that if Krushchev shot in place of Kennedy, we can agree at least that Mrs Krushchev will not marry Aristotle Onassis.

A little laughter. Silence. Then:

HASIM. Actually . . . I am also in America at this time. In New York for colloquium of legal implications of treatment of HIV.

This sounds potentially threatening.

GINA. Is this / something that affects –

HASIM. And there is good joke told there also.

Unnoticed, JAN *enters with his water.*

Why does New York get all lawyers and San Francisco all homosexual? And answer is: San Francisco gets first pick.

ROMAN, NIKOLAI, ERIK *and* GINA *laugh, interrupted by:*

JAN. Oh, *right.* I see.

HASIM. What?

JAN. It's the same as why the Arabs get the oil and Gezhekhs get the turnips.

NIKOLAI. Uh . . .

JAN. Because . . .

He picks up that this may not be a good idea as:

KELIMA. . . . like San Franciscans, Gezhekhs will choose first.

JAN. Yes.

KELIMA. It is often told about Drozhdans and brown coal.

NIKOLAI *(attempted rescue).* Hey. How you define moral dilemma for Kavkhazian. Your customer pay you thousand lek note in place of a 500. The dilemma – do you tell your partner?

HASIM *(not good enough).* Ah yes, of course. 'Tactic of souk'.

An edgy moment. ROMAN *decides to deflect:*

ROMAN. But the Russians have the best joke. A man from the south applies for a good job. The Russian says, this is all fine, you seem most excellently qualified, but there is just

one thing. Where do you come from? And the man says, oh,
I am Drozhdanian. And the Russian says, oh dear, I'm sorry,
this is an obstacle we cannot surmount, as everybody knows
the Drozhdanians are very very lazy. And the man says, no,
no, it's OK. You've got it wrong. It's the Kavkhazians that
are very lazy. The Drozhdanians are crooks.

HASIM. Ah yes of course. This is like Drozhdani father who
has son who comes one day and says, father I want to marry
Kavkhaz girl, and her father says, this is terrible, you want
your kids to be too dumb to steal?

Angry, KELIMA *stands and goes to get another sandwich.*

But maybe joke offend our company.

NIKOLAI. Particularly not exclusively our hostess.

GINA. Oh I am not offended.

NIKOLAI. Good.

The wind has gone out of the moment. KELIMA *sits.
Another silence.*

GINA. But it shows the problem does it not? If you cannot
make your minds up whether your neighbours are more
dishonest than they're lazy than they're dumb.

Pause. Everyone is taken aback by GINA*'s aggression.*

ERIK. But of course, a joke can often represent / a deeper
truth –

GINA. And as everyone points out you have been here three
days, and everyone agrees we must find common ground
because the alternative to finding it is yet more sons and
husbands dying pointlessly, and yet more wives and
daughters too. But of course how can you find a
compromise which inevitably must rely on trust with people
who faced with choosing between war and peace choose
bloodshed as first pick?

Slight pause.

But maybe I make too big a point of something that is actually very trivial. After all, what do they say about the Finns?

NIKOLAI. What do they say?

HASIM. No sense of humour.

GINA. I am so sorry. We did our best. We are down to the difference between two words. I can't see what else we can do. Come, Jan, let's go to bed.

KELIMA *intervenes.*

KELIMA. I have a joke. In 1944 when Drozhdan people are expel by Stalin to Khazakhstan. And whole villages of lazy Drozhdanis dumped in middle of marshy land where no cattle graze and no wheat may grow. And Russians say, that's that. But since five year they come back and behold Drozhdans have plant rice and fed themselves. So Russians take all rice and transport Drozhdans to great height mountain where they put them down to die. But still Drozhdans maybe too stupid still to comprehend and they build igloo and kill mountain bear to eat. And five year is pass and Russians come back once again, and Drozhdans still alive so smash their igloo and move all Drozhdan to baking desert. And again behold, stupid idle Drozhdans raise goat and feed off meat and milk and when three year is pass and Russians come back and say, Look. If these dumb idle Drozhdans still survive, now maybe we send them all back home. And so / at last they go back –

ROMAN *comes quickly in.*

ROMAN. Of course. They get back home to find their farms are occupied since 1944 by wicked Kavkhars and their house is smashed up and their livestock dead. And yes what happen to the Drozhdan people is most terrible. But they are not the only people who will suffer then or now.

KELIMA. Well so you say.

ROMAN. Well so I say.

KELIMA. But it is not quite what I hear.

Slight pause.

ROMAN. Oh no?

KELIMA. I hear . . . you are from Sukhidat. Maybe your
parent or your grandparent are ones who occupy a
Drozhdan flat or farm.

ROMAN. Maybe.

KELIMA. And maybe they don't smash it up at all, but leave
it clean, with bread and salt upon the table for those who
return. And who knows perhaps despite this Drozhdan
children who are tired and starving from their journey maybe
still they call your grandmother bad names and spit at her.

ROMAN. You know that these things happened.

KELIMA. And when she get a new flat or farm it is OK but
smaller, soil a little thinner, a little further off from town.

Pause.

And I hear you say: 'OK, my grandmother she does not
suffer quite so much as yours. But she suffer still. And now
she is – 80? 85? – she sit alone and think what happens
now if children and grandchildren of those Drozhdans win
their independence. What will happen to her now?' Is this
not what I hear?

ROMAN. Of course.

Pause.

And you say this. 'Fifty years ago, it is hard between us but
it is not so bad as now. Now you say: We cannot speak our
language to our children. Now you exclude us from all civil
life and hospitals and schools. After everything you do to
us, is it any wonder that you cannot trust us not to kill your
grandmother? So please dear Mr Litvinyenko, how may we
convince you you are wrong?'

Pause.

GINA. You know the choice. It's possible that either side will
win. It's possible – it's likely – if you go home now your
two communities can sit and scowl across the Bela while
the sanctions squeeze away. But surely there's a better
option for both sides.

ROMAN (*to* KELIMA). And of course I hear you when you say you cannot 'renounce' the only tactic open to you.

Slight pause.

But maybe now you may reject it.

KELIMA. 'Reject' imply it is not happening I think.

ROMAN. That's true.

ERIK. So then if not 'reject', 'forsake'?

HASIM *looks to* KELIMA.

GINA. Or if not 'forsake', 'relinquish'?

Slight pause.

Voluntary. Not conceding rights or principles. Not implying it was wrong before.

HASIM *looks up to* KELIMA.

KELIMA. We can accept 'relinquish'. Yes. Agreed. What next?

JAN *looks questioningly at his mother.* ERIK *smiles.*
NIKOLAI *looks at the document.* GINA *nods to her son.*

Scene Six

Three months later. Geneva. The hall in Geneva airport prepared for a ceremony. Two small tables with flags, a lectern with the crest of the US Secretary of State. Logos of the OSCE, the EU, the UN and the Governments of Finland and Switzerland on hangings behind. Two ORDERLIES *are setting out chairs.* PATTERSON, *now 39, is checking what they're doing against a chart in his hand. He is also talking on a mobile telephone.*

PATTERSON. OK. Do you have an atlas? Open it at Europe. Can you find Italy? Place your finger on the bottom and go upwards, there's a kind of oval bit that may be brown or squiggly to indicate it's mountainous, and a little blue smudge, with the word 'Geneva'. Beside which is a little airplane in a circle. That's where we are.

He reangles a pair of chairs. The ORDERLIES *notice this.*

Now take your finger rightwards to Vienna – it's possible it may be spelt W – I – E – N. *You bet* on purpose. And thence to Budapest – you have that? – then to Bucharest, yuh, you'd think they'd make them sound more different, and then the Black Sea which is strictly neither, *then . . .* you got it.

He notices the flags on the table. Picks it up. To an ORDERLY:

Hey. There's a no flag rule.

The ORDERLY *looks blank.* PATTERSON *tries German:*

PATTERSON (*German*). Keine Fahnen! [No flags!].

1st ORDERLY (*French*). Je parle Français. Nous sommes à Genève. [I speak French. This is Geneva.]

PATTERSON (*French*). Nous avons convenu. Pas de drapeaux. [There's an agreement, no flags.]

1st ORDERLY (*French*). D'accord. [Fine.]

The 1st ORDERLY *takes the flags out.*

PATTERSON. But I understand the stationery is subtly colour-coded.

Checking on his chart:

Oh. And the wrong way round.

Down the phone:

No, it's your dime.

Slight pause. PATTERSON *changing the pens, blotters and agreement binders round, as he speaks:*

Two reasons. One, the deal was done in Finland, so the alternative to Geneva is the Outokumpu Declaration and it was felt to be in the interests of amity for it to be proclaimed somewhere the signatories could pronounce.

To the 2nd ORDERLY, *in French, as the* 1st ORDERLY *returns:*

Hey, are there not supposed to be some flowers? (*French*).
N'y a-t-il pas de fleurs? [Aren't there flowers?]

2nd ORDERLY (*Italian*). Prego? [Excuse me?]

PATTERSON (*French, to the other* ORDERLY). N'y a-t-il pas
de fleurs? [Aren't there flowers?].

1st ORDERLY. I hear you. They will come.

PATTERSON (*down phone*). While second, we're passing
through en route from the conclusion of the Peace of
Amman to the initialling of the Amsterdam Accords.

Enter KELIMA. *She is dressed formally. She has a plastic
information pack issued for the day.*

Brain dead, frankly, though I didn't say that.

Oh, no. Our role in this is essentially ceremonial. Didn't
you hear? We are in the Hour of Europe.

Sure. Again.

Handing a chair to the 1st ORDERLY:

I think you'll find the Gezekh Consul has a wheelchair.

1st ORDERLY. Fine.

The ORDERLIES *go out.*

PATTERSON. No, that's not you. No, in this case, you can
take it that I *am* the Secretary of State.

He snaps his phone shut. To KELIMA:

Major US media. Talk about spoonfed.

KELIMA. I am Kelima Bejta.

PATTERSON*'s phone goes.*

PATTERSON. Excuse me.

PATTERSON *answers his phone.*

KELIMA. Drozhdan People's Front.

PATTERSON (*down phone*). No, it's all agreed, no speeches.
They'll just have to issue press releases just like everybody
else.

Phone off. To KELIMA*:*

Sorry. Pat Davis. You're here for the handshake.

KELIMA. Yes.

PATTERSON *puts out his hand.*

PATTERSON. Well, hi.

KELIMA. Uh, in fact, you are . . . ?

PATTERSON*'s phone goes.*

PATTERSON. Oh heck.

He answers the phone:

Hi. No. He's General Secretary. So it's 'Mr General Secretary'. Then 'Mr Secretary'.

Snaps phone shut. To KELIMA*:*

Sorry. 'In fact, I am'?

KELIMA. I understand there would be . . . other people.

Enter GINA*, also smartly dressed for the ceremony, with her pack.*

PATTERSON. Sure, and so there are. Hey. Gina *Olsson.*

GINA. Well, Patterson. You've come some way.

PATTERSON*'s phone rings.*

PATTERSON. You too. One second.

Down phone:

What?

KELIMA. Secretary of State?

GINA. Um . . .

PATTERSON. I'm *on hold*?

GINA. Why don't you switch that off.

PATTERSON. Hey. Great idea.

He switches off his phone.

GINA. Is this the handshake?

PATTERSON (*approaching her*). Yes this is the handshake.

GINA. I thought, the Secretary of State . . .

KELIMA. This is not Secretary of State?

PATTERSON. As if.

KELIMA. 'I *am* the Secretary of State'.

PATTERSON. Ah. I mean, I am speaking for the Secretary of
    State. As opposed to a state department spokesman, or a
    'senior state department source'. Or indeed 'a source close
    to the Secretary of State'. Which actually is the Secretary of
    State. Who proceeds here from the Sheraton in precisely
    one hour seven minutes time. To preside benignly over the
    historic handshake between the General Secretary of the
    Drozhdan People's Front and President Y.V. Petrovian of the
    Republic of Kavkhazia.

GINA. One hour?

PATTERSON. Pretty nearly.

GINA (*realises*). Central Europe summer time.

KELIMA. Excuse please. You two know each other?

GINA. Yes. We met at the same seminar where I meet Kolya
    Shubkin.

PATTERSON. At which point Miss Olsson is somewhere to
    the left of Kim Il Sung.

KELIMA (*to* GINA *then* PATTERSON). I see. So what is
    brain dead?

PATTERSON. What?

KELIMA. You say something is brain dead. On the telephone.
    But you 'didn't say it'.

PATTERSON. Ah. The Amsterdam Accords.

GINA. Not this.

PATTERSON. No, of course not. How's the hotel?

KELIMA. I am not yet in hotel. I am only just arrive.

GINA *looks questioningly.*

PATTERSON. There was a problem with Miss Bejta's visa. Then when we think we've got our ducks all in a row the Kavkhars try to stiff us with a change in the agreement.

GINA. What?

She looks in her well-stuffed information pack.

KELIMA. It is after map and welcome of President of Switzerland.

GINA. What is the problem?

KELIMA. They are suddenly so unhappy with 'acknowledging the DPF as legitimate representative'.

GINA (*she's found it*). Well, we know that. That's why we changed 'the legitimate' to 'a legitimate'.

PATTERSON. In a country without definite or indefinite articles. Boy.

GINA. Ah. 'Recognises the DPF as a acknowledged representative of the Drozhdan people'.

KELIMA. We give them 'legitimate' to 'acknowledged' in exchange for 'acknowledge' to 'recognise'.

PATTERSON. And forgot to change the 'a' to 'an'.

KELIMA. Good deal, we thought.

PATTERSON. Me too.

GINA. So where is everybody else?

Slight pause.

PATTERSON. So. Is there not a Mr Olsson?

GINA. His name is Trask. He is not here.

PATTERSON (*taking out his phone and dialling*). Oh? I'd better let him know.

He looks at his phone.

KELIMA. You switch it off.

GINA. Who know?

PATTERSON. Hey, right.

He switches it on. Checking against his chart, he goes to a distant part of the room and removes a chair.

The Secretary of State. I think he'd worked out some light diplomatic joke about 'who wears the striped pants here'.

He's dialling.

GINA. Well, we must be grateful for small mercies.

PATTERSON. Hey, he does his best.

GINA. So this is where I am sitting?

PATTERSON. Sure. Oh, by the way, he is left-handed. And whatever he calls you, you call him 'Mr Secretary'.

He's through.

Hi. Yuh, I switched it off. Ain't that the truth.

Oh, courtesy, you know?

Pause.

OK. Yuh, sure. I'll be right there.

Snaps phone shut.

KELIMA. Problem?

PATTERSON. Well, yes. In the sense of 'no'. In the sense of – well, we're running late. But apart from that, everything is . . . fine and dandy.

Nervy pause.

Hey do you know the original idea of handshakes is to demonstrate there's nothing in your hand.

He goes out. The women look at each other, deciding not to speculate as to what PATTERSON *has heard on the phone.*

KELIMA. So. Erik does not come?

GINA. No. He says it is 'my moment'.

KELIMA. But everything I so much hope is 'fine and dandy'.

Very slight pause.

GINA. Oh, completely. Um . . . Drozdhani colours, I presume?

KELIMA. That's right.

GINA. You look most elegant.

KELIMA. You sound surprise.

GINA. No, I'm sorry. Why shouldn't you look elegant.

KELIMA. Just because I am major terrorist by regular daytime employment.

GINA. But we hope not for too much longer.

KELIMA. If so because of you.

GINA. Oh, no.

KELIMA. Hey. You may settle now a question. Majdani and I think you get so angry with all jokes, so everyone think, hey, at least we have one thing in common, unlike dour Miss Finland, at least we all have sense of humour. Is this not correct?

Pause.

GINA. Yes, you're correct.

KELIMA. Then maybe I am right about another little thing.

GINA. Oh, what?

KELIMA. That when I ask if everything is fine and dandy in your life, and you say 'Oh completely', it is in the sense of 'maybe not quite absolutely', no?

GINA *takes out a packet of cigarettes.*

GINA. Well, I'm sure we're not supposed to smoke.

KELIMA. You smoke?

GINA. Very rarely. Not at home. Do you want one?

KELIMA. No. I give it up. Your good example.

Slight pause.

So. Again. My question?

GINA *lights up.*

GINA. You know how tiresome it can be when people claim political activity is just a way of masking problems in your private life. As no doubt they say you are a revolutionary because your borders were invaded as a child.

KELIMA. My borders *are* invaded.

GINA. I meant, your personal . . . The theory that, if you're abused . . .

KELIMA. Of course. Or you want a husband really.

GINA. Or to kill your father.

KELIMA. Or to have a child.

Slight pause.

GINA. And do you?

Pause.

KELIMA. My hope above all things is that today will come to pass.

Slight pause.

GINA. Now, do you get the feeling / something's going on –

GINA*'s mobile phone rings.* GINA *answers it.*

GINA. Hallo? Allo.

In French:

Non, je n'ai pas vu de télévision. Dois-je? [No I haven't seen a television. Should I?]

KELIMA *takes out her mobile. But before she gets to dial, she sees that* ROMAN *has entered, dark and formal in his suit.*

GINA. Roman.

ROMAN. Here you are.

GINA. What's happening?

ROMAN. So no one's told you.

KELIMA. What?

GINA (*French*). Je te rappelerai. [I'll call you back.]

KELIMA. What's happens?

GINA (*shutting off her phone*). What happens is that the Kavkhars have pulled out of the agreement.

ROMAN. Yes.

KELIMA. What?

ROMAN. As a consequence of a violation of the terms of the ceasefire.

GINA. Some Drozhdani kids pick up a police clerk . . .

ROMAN. Well, they take him hostage. As retaliation for a police raid on a Fiore club which claim to be Islamic centre but police say front for drugs.

KELIMA. Oh, and naturally/ everybody is arrested –

ROMAN. And so yesterday off-duty policeman's kidnapped. And by the time he is release Drozhdani Kavkhars occupy assembly in Fiore demanding that agreement is abort.

KELIMA. To which provocation doubtless Petrovian gives in.

ROMAN. No, actually he orders the army to retake the building. It is his generals who refuse. Not least because a Kavkhar group called the Society for St Demetrius organises for 500 people to be lying on the steps.

GINA. But the police guy is released?

ROMAN. Oh yes.

KELIMA. And he is harmed?

ROMAN. No, he is not. But by / this time . . .

GINA. And the agreement?

ROMAN. I overhear the black guy say – 'game over'.

GINA. But they can't do that.

ROMAN. They've done it.

GINA. And the Secretary of State?

ROMAN. Apparently he is held hostage by world press in Sheraton. They are busy try to find a way to slip him out.

GINA. O God.

ROMAN. I'm sorry.

GINA. So am I.

They both look at KELIMA. KELIMA *goes and picks up the duty-free bag she brought in. She holds it out to* GINA.

KELIMA. I buy this for you. Celebration of big mountain which we climb. Don't worry, it is not ashtray.

She turns to ROMAN.

Lie one. Beneath, we all the same. Lie two, an unjust peace is always better than a just war. Lie three, of course, that this is spontaneous action by Society of St Demetrius.

She goes out. GINA *is left there with the bag.*

GINA. The check is in the mail. My husband doesn't understand me.

ROMAN. And the common ground is big enough for everyone.

GINA. What do you mean?

ROMAN. Room enough for us, of course. Those who enjoy fine food, fine wine, fine conversation. But problem is the people that are leave behind. The Islamic Centre and the Society for St Demetrius. So-called 'extremists' on both sides. And so Pandora's Doll is blow apart.

Slight pause.

GINA. So is it true? That Petrovian set up this demonstration?

ROMAN. Look, the guy was just a police clerk. I don't think he even wore a uniform.

GINA. Nothing happened to him.

ROMAN. But he doesn't know that, until it has not happened.
Tied, blindfold, terrified, doubtless threatened and abused in
a language that he doesn't understand. In fact, of course, it
is much worse before. When you don't know what they'll
do to you.

Slight pause.

GINA. 'In fact'.

ROMAN. That's right. In fact.

Pause.

They think because of this I make no compromise. That
I am hardcop of all hardcop, because of what the Drozhdans
do to me. But I realise that like us Drozhdan are divided and
unsure of what to do. Which makes me even more
determined to succeed.

GINA. What was your experience?

ROMAN. Oh not too terrible. They decided I am a better
messenger than martyr. And the message was – let's build
the bridge we burn today.

He stands, goes to the doorway, turns back.

You have a fear. That you discover real problem with your
search for common ground. That when people see it they
don't want it. As so nice Miss Bejta say. Not that we do not
know each other. But that we know each other all too well.

*He goes out. GINA sits and looks at the empty chairs and
tables around her. She opens the airport bag, looks inside.
She closes the bag, looks upwards, closes her eyes. Then she
takes out her mobile phone and dials.*

GINA. Kelima, it's . . .

She realises it's an answermessage.

OK. It's Gina. Just to say . . . All I can ask you, is to believe
this thing was worth it. That it will happen, if not now, then
in the future. That we will – climb the mountain once again,

to find our common ground. And if there is the faintest prospect of that happening, I promise I'll do anything to make it come to pass.

She clicks the phone shut, opens the bag, takes out a tube of Toblerone, unwraps it and bites off a piece. NIKOLAI *enters to* GINA, *late, in his suit, with his suitcase and a huge bouquet of flowers. He sees* GINA, *her mouth full of Swiss chocolate.*

NIKOLAI. Miss Gina Olsson. So where is everybody else?

GINA (*wiping her mouth*). They ratted.

End of Act One.

ACT TWO

'A second requirement of a potential settlement
is that it is Pareto optimal. This condition is fulfilled
for settlement A if no alternative settlement B exists
such that at least one party is better off with B than with A,
while at the same time no party is worse off with B
than with A.'

Jon Hovi
Games, Threats and Treaties, 1998

'The Americans thought a few meetings would solve it,
as if it were a personal quarrel. In reality, we were divided
by a mountain of corpses.'

Aliya Izetbegovic
President of Bosnia, 1995

'The Chechen–Ingush Republic is a sovereign state,
created as a result of the self-determination of
the Chechen and Ingush peoples . . . The Chechen–Ingush
Republic has the attributes of a sovereign state:
citizenship, a crest, a flag, a national anthem and a capital.'

Declaration of Chechen Congress,
November 1992

'I am the President. I am His Excellency, the President
of Palestine. What you want to do is make me
the head man of a village council.'

Yasser Arafat,
December 1993

'The US military is committed to a doctrine
that entertains military intervention only when a massive
preponderance of force can be brought to bear with clear
political objectives and a defined endpoint.'

Bill Clinton,
Presidential Directive 25 (PDD-25), 1994

'In the First World War, over 80 per cent of battlefield deaths
were combatants; by the 1990s over 90 per cent
of war-related deaths are civilians, killed in their own homes
and communities . . . The least dangerous place
to be in most contemporary wars is the military'.

Miall, Ramsbotham and Woodhouse
Contemporary Conflict Resolution, 1999

ACT TWO

Scene One

*Two years later. Drozhdan/Drozhdevnya. Summer. A checkpoint
on the edge of government-held territory. A large cube of
medical supplies stands upstage, marked with the Aid Express
logo. It has been broken into, with boxes opened and packs
and even pill boxes opened to check on their contents, left on
the ground. LEN, a Black British UN soldier in his 30s, is
keeping his eye on the boxes, watched warily by a*
KAVKHAZIAN SOLDIER. *A* 2nd KAVKHAZIAN SOLDIER
comes in to speak with him. Downstage, FLOSS *waits. Enter*
NIKOLAI SHUBKIN, *in field military uniform. He has papers.*

NIKOLAI. Well why Miss Weatherby.

FLOSS *turns.*

FLOSS. Ah good afternoon. Are you the commanding / officer –

NIKOLAI. But this is disappointing very much.

FLOSS. I beg your pardon?

NIKOLAI. You clearly do not readily remember me.

FLOSS. Uh . . . no?

NIKOLAI. My name is Shubkin. Last time we meet in
University Santa Cruz.

FLOSS. Oh . . . yes. At the peace seminar.

NIKOLAI. How all things turn about.

FLOSS. Ain't that the truth.

NIKOLAI. In fact, not for first time. Since two years I am with
Miss Gina Olsson of Finland in hush hush backstage
negotiations.

FLOSS. Yes, I know. They failed.

NIKOLAI. Yes, sadly.

FLOSS. I understand that she was very disappointed.

NIKOLAI. I am very disappointed also.

FLOSS. Professor Shubkin / we need to talk about –

NIKOLAI. But now here it is, we meet inside this crazy
    situations. And charming Mr Neil from Dublin Town also.
    What place for class reunion.

FLOSS. 'Mr Neil'?

NIKOLAI. So they are telling me.

FLOSS. Who's telling you?

> NIKOLAI *waves his papers. They are faxes. During this the*
> 2nd KAVKHAZIAN SOLDIER *goes out.*

NIKOLAI. Our people naturally fax copy of your passport.
    You may think this very primitive. Once we are scanning all
    such thing and sending digitally from mobile phone. Sadly
    since five month terrorist have track equipment from Iran
    which mean you are on satellite for more than minute plus a
    half and boom. This of course in quite watertight major
    international arms embargo. Now I am right that Aid
    Express is once call Helping Hand?

FLOSS. That's right.

NIKOLAI. New name more hip and up-to-date.

FLOSS. Well, yes. Professor Shubkin / are you in charge –

NIKOLAI. Colonel, but please, Kolya.

FLOSS. Are you in charge of these men here?

NIKOLAI. I am in charge of many men. Now maybe you
    please tell me now of what is situation.

FLOSS. As you are aware, Aid Express is an accredited aid
    body supported by the UN, transporting desperately needed
    medical supplies to Estafan.

NIKOLAI. Of course. Maybe I question little bit so desperate need.

FLOSS. And this mission has full authorisation from the Kavkhaz high command.

NIKOLAI. Of course I know this. I am part of Kavkhaz high command.

FLOSS. And that this consignment has sat here for eight hours in the heat being so-called 'checked' by so-called 'tax officials' – all of whom went off at least an hour ago to 'telephone for fresh instructions', all because these men – your men – refuse to let supplies through to the people who, yes, desperately need them.

NIKOLAI. And why is this?

FLOSS. You know full well. Because you want the Drozhdans to release a group of ethnic Kavkhazians whose presence in Estafan is effectively the population's only guarantee of safety from your guns. A solution neither to our liking nor frankly in our gift.

NIKOLAI. Even though this happen often now in both direction. Even though three day ago we let 200 Muslim wife and children free from Novye Ghla.

FLOSS. Yes I am aware of what occurred in Novye Ghla.

NIKOLAI. But you do not prefer be ethnic cleansing aid assistant.

FLOSS. No, frankly not.

NIKOLAI. You wish instead all people here to live in peace and harmony and love is all you need.

FLOSS. Colonel Shubkin, this is not a time / for jokes –

NIKOLAI. No, I agree. But in this time I fear Miss Weatherby you are quite way behind.

Slight pause. He looks at his watch.

Since – hour plus thirty minute, terrorist leadership agree to our quite reasonable request to evacuation of innocent civilians. Convoy approach. All sorted. No one is telling you?

FLOSS. What? It's all sorted?

NIKOLAI. From our point of view.

FLOSS. Why, is there a problem with the other side?

NIKOLAI. In such cases always glitch is possible.

FLOSS. And the convoy's on its way?

NIKOLAI. Of course. Now I remember. Floss.

Slight pause.

FLOSS. Yes.

NIKOLAI. Short for 'Florence'.

FLOSS. Yes.

NIKOLAI (*looks at fax*). But in full, Miss Florence Hazel
Weatherby.

Slight pause.

In Russia middle name for father. Maybe Hazel name your
mother?

FLOSS. It's my aunt. My elder sister has my mother's name.

NIKOLAI. But if you very close friend with Nikolai then he
call 'Kolya'. As if you close friend with Florence you may
call her maybe Floss.

FLOSS. Well, yes. Of course.

Slight pause.

Now, the consignment . . .

*Enter JAMES NEIL followed by a 33-year old aid worker,
TREVELYAN, the group's 24-year-old translator, EMELA,
and the* 2nd KAVKHAZIAN SOLDIER.

JAMES. Floss, this is intolerable.

FLOSS. Trev. What's happening?

TREVELYAN. They've heard back from 'headquarters'.
Apparently, they have to take it all apart.

NIKOLAI. So maybe now glitch come.

FLOSS. What, all of it?

JAMES. And if there's one pack or tablet over . . .

NIKOLAI. Well, why Mr Neil. Long time no see.

JAMES. Uh – yes?

NIKOLAI. From Dublin Town.

JAMES looks to FLOSS.

FLOSS. It's Professor Shubkin.

NIKOLAI (*puts out his hand*). Well it since many years back naturally.

JAMES. Professor?

FLOSS. Colonel. But – but still.

JAMES. Ah. Right. Right. Well.

Discommoded, he shakes NIKOLAI's hand.

TREVELYAN. Colonel, your men are demanding that they take the delivery apart, so they can 'inspect it', and it would be very helpful if you could tell them / that this is inter-ference with an authorised humanitarian consignment . . .

NIKOLAI (*to* 2nd KAVKHAZIAN, *in Kavkhaz*). Kakvó stáva took? [What's going on?]

2nd KAVKHAZIAN (*Kavkhaz*). Tryábva da naprávim revíziya na kartónite s taká naréchenata 'houmanitárna pómosht'. [We need to inspect the so-called 'medical supplies'.]

NIKOLAI (*Kavkhaz*). Sufsém priémlivo e. A te otkázvat? [Sounds reasonable enough. And they refuse?]

2nd KAVKHAZIAN (*Kavkhaz*). Tézi hóra sa mnógo ópaki. [These people are not reasonable.]

JAMES (*to* EMELA). Well?

EMELA. He ask what is big issue here. He say: We wish to search the so-called medical supplies. He say: Sounds reasonable to me. So what's the problem? He reply: These people are not reasonable.

NIKOLAI (*Kavkhaz*). Razbírate li kafkázki? [You understand Kavkhaz?]

EMELA. A little.

NIKOLAI (*Kavkhaz*). Áma víe anglichánka ste? [But you are English?]

EMELA. I live now in England.

NIKOLAI. And your name?

EMELA. Emela.

NIKOLAI. Ah. So many Drozhdan western passport. Sometimes it seem compulsory.

EMELA. My mother is Drozhdani. My father is originally from Baku. I am language student now since three years at Bristol England. Now I work you see for Aid Express.

NIKOLAI. I make just general point. I understand that DPF high command consist of weightlifter who defect to USA at Seoul Olympics, pharmacologist who work in New York driving minicab since five years and barman voted number one at cocktail shaking three years running by some most important London magazine. While so-call Drozhdan so-call Ambassador to European Union live in Paris on proceeds of narcotics prostitution and arm smuggling and has not set foot here since he is small baby.

JAMES. I am not, I have to say, that interested in all of this.

NIKOLAI. Oh, no? It is for these people you deliver medical supplies.

TREVELYAN. No not those people.

NIKOLAI. Ah. You think they all end up with sick and wounded lying now in hospital.

JAMES. Well, not if your men have their way.

NIKOLAI. Once more I think that like Miss Weatherby you way behind. Happily our demand are met. Our citizens are now release. Just when they will be here, you may deliver your supply.

JAMES *looks at* FLOSS *who nods.*

JAMES. What, unconditionally?

FLOSS. Seems so.

NIKOLAI. Only naturally subject to inspection.

TREVELYAN. Oh, right.

JAMES. Oh I see. You mean as soon as you've ripped off what you want then you will graciously allow us to deliver the remainder to the sick and dying.

FLOSS. James.

NIKOLAI *is angry.*

JAMES. Well, what d'you think / that this is all about –

TREVELYAN. Jim, let it go.

FLOSS. Hear hear.

NIKOLAI (*to 2nd* KAVKHAZIAN SOLDIER, *in Kavkhaz*). Ímate li spíssuka na sudurzhánieto na kartónite? [Do you have the manifest?]

2nd KAVKHAZIAN (*Kavkhaz*). Éto. [Here it is.]

As NIKOLAI *looks at the manifest.*

JAMES. Here we go again. Just like at Kudjali.

FLOSS. Well, this is Kavkhazia.

EMELA. He reads the manifest.

NIKOLAI (*Kavkhaz*). Kakvó e [What is] 'anti-histamine'?

2nd KAVKHAZIAN (*Kavkhaz*). Ne znam. [I don't know.]

Simultaneous with:

JAMES. I don't see why we should make involuntary donations.

FLOSS. Don't you?

JAMES. Why, do you?

FLOSS. Yes, when we're nearly there.

NIKOLAI (*Kavkhaz*). Da, imenáta zvouchát káto meditsínski. [Well, it all sounds plausibly medical.]

EMELA. He seems convinced.

NIKOLAI. Washing powder? Washing powder is a medical supply?

TREVELYAN. Yes of course it is. If you're in a lice and rat-infested hospital without power or water / then obviously –

NIKOLAI. But I am quite content this medicine will be deliver now.

FLOSS. You are?

NIKOLAI. As gesture of goodwill and trust for two old friend.

His mobile phone rings. He answers. In Kavkhaz:

Álo, Shóubkin na telefóna. [Hallo, this is Shubkin.] (*English.*) Ah. Hallo. How good to hear you. Yes of course. So I expect. Where are the buses? Yes so we do same thing at Novye Ghla. Of course I understand.

End call.

Another old friend comes her way.

(*To* 2nd KAVKHAZIAN SOLDIER, *Kavkhaz*) Ídvat. Vurvéte da gi posréshtnete. [They're coming. Go and meet them.]

2nd KAVKHAZIAN (*Kavkhaz*). Slóusham goospoodíneh. [Yes, sir.]

He goes out. TREVELYAN *goes to speak to* LEN, *the UN soldier.*

FLOSS. Thank you.

NIKOLAI *looks to* JAMES.

JAMES. Yes, thanks.

NIKOLAI. You're welcome.

Slight pause.

So Florence-Floss. And what you playing at since all these years go by?

FLOSS. Oh, you know. This. Trying to be helpful without getting killed.

NIKOLAI. But James when we last meet you will be government advisor?

JAMES. Sure. I was persuaded to change course.

NIKOLAI. By maybe Florence Weatherby?

JAMES. Yes, as it happens.

NIKOLAI. And you maybe married now?

FLOSS. What, to each other?

NIKOLAI. Well . . .

JAMES. No, we're neither of us married.

FLOSS. And, I can't remember . . .

NIKOLAI. My wife she die since one year and one half. Something go bad from small operation in her ear.

FLOSS. I'm sorry.

NIKOLAI. So since I fail to solve my country problems, now I must try to keep him in one piece.

JAMES. That's how you see it?

NIKOLAI. Like US Civil War. 'One nation under God.'

FLOSS. But surely, that's the problem.

NIKOLAI. Surely. Two nationality, two religion, two language and two alphabet. Sadly, one range of mountain, one big river, one coastline and one coal field, one electric grid. Even now we do big deal with Volkswagen for nickel alloy and smart guy from Texaco find perfect route for Baku crude to run through Kavkhaz pipeline to Black Sea. But yet without we agree we split our country up from top to bottom, NATO send you people home and bomb us back to stone age.

JAMES. Well, that's not quite how / I'd put it –

NIKOLAI. But maybe Mr Neil think we so primitive barbarian we in stone age time already.

JAMES. No of course I don't.

NIKOLAI. It is believe all Drozhdan women work for foreign NGOs are prostitute. Also that all UN troop from Africa have HIV. I fight against these most unprogressive view.

FLOSS. Len isn't African. He comes from Lewisham.

NIKOLAI. Ah Star Wars Two.

FLOSS. Beg pardon?.

NIKOLAI. The Empire Strike You Back.

Enter the 2nd KAVKHAZIAN SOLDIER.

2nd KAVKHAZIAN (*Kavkhaz*). Slézoha ot dzhípa i ídvat. [They are coming from their fourwheel.]

Both KAVKHAZIAN SOLDIERS *aiming guns at the entering group:* KELIMA, *in paramilitary uniform, and a small family: a* FATHER, MOTHER, *wheeling a* YOUNG MAN *in a wheelchair and a 10-year-old* BOY.

KELIMA. Nikolai Mikhailovich.

NIKOLAI. Kelima Bejta. You bring us sample group in fourwheel.

KELIMA. Yes.

She goes to shake his hand. The 2nd KAVKHAZIAN SOLDIER *stops her.*

What's this?

2nd KAVKHAZIAN (*Kavkhaz*). Tryábva da ya pretúrsim. [We should search her.]

NIKOLAI. He wants to search you.

KELIMA. The idea of handshake is to show that you have nothing in your hand. But fine. Maybe you search your people also. Maybe you start with guy in wheelchair.

NIKOLAI (*taking the point*). OK.

2nd KAVKHAZIAN (*Kavkhaz*). Pokazhéte ni poné váshata líchna kárta. [At least we must see your papers.]

NIKOLAI. He say . . .

KELIMA. Yes, I know. Sure. They your people. Naturally they have ID.

NIKOLAI (*Kavkhaz, to the* SOLDIER). Da, preglédaite dokouméntite im. [Yes, check their papers.]

The 2nd KAVKHAZIAN SOLDIER *goes to look at the family's papers.* TREVELYAN *is returning to the main group.*

JAMES (*to* FLOSS). So where are all the others?

NIKOLAI. They keep in bus as hostage. As I will do just the same.

KELIMA *hands him binoculars. He looks offstage.*

FLOSS. Hostage for what?

JAMES. The consignment, we must hope.

KELIMA. And also till we cut our deal.

NIKOLAI. What deal?

TREVELYAN. What's this?

FLOSS. Don't know.

NIKOLAI. We have deal already. You release our people, there is medical delivery.

KELIMA. We need more things besides.

Slight pause.

NIKOLAI. What?

KELIMA. Diesel.

NIKOLAI. Diesel?

JAMES. Oh for Christ's sake . . .

FLOSS. Look do you mean / you won't –

KELIMA. I mean there is no point in medicine if no heat or light. So we cannot accept medical consignment.

JAMES. You can't *accept* it?

KELIMA. Luckily our generator run on diesel power. Presumably you must have diesel.

JAMES. So are you saying that you won't / accept the consignment –

FLOSS. James, it's clear enough what she's saying.

NIKOLAI. But I'm sorry this not possible.

KELIMA. Well it most clearly *possible* . . .

NIKOLAI. As last time we are let in diesel surprise surprise it is not use in hospital but for military purpose.

KELIMA (*to* FLOSS). This of course gross propaganda / and most typical –

NIKOLAI. No, gross propaganda is you move all patient to one hospital and invite on CNN. Gross propaganda is you fire big mortar round from hospital courtyard so returning fire seem like unprovoked attack on innocent civilian.

KELIMA. This quite typical as lies. You read it on their website.

NIKOLAI. Propaganda is when hospital / is use as front for –

JAMES. Can I just clear this up. You are saying you will not *receive* this medicine unless / the Kavkhazian army agrees –

FLOSS. Yes, James, that is what she means.

NIKOLAI. This is most typical of Drozhdan.

FLOSS (*to* JAMES, *an order*). They're playing chicken and we're playing prisoner's dilemma.

NIKOLAI. So maybe now I say no deal? We keep your medicine?

FLOSS. You see?

KELIMA *gestures at the family.*

KELIMA. And we turn bus round about and drive off home.
And tell Radio Liberty and BBC how much you care for
your trapped people.

Pause.

NIKOLAI. OK. I call HQ.

He takes out his mobile phone.

KELIMA. Hey, you make long call on cellphone? Boy.

NIKOLAI. OK. I go use radio.

He makes to go as the 2nd KAVKHAZIAN SOLDIER
*comes up to him with one of the IDs of the family. He takes
him aside a little beyond* EMELA*'s hearing.*

2nd KAVKHAZIAN (*Kavkhaz*). Goospoodín polkóvnik,
sumnyávam se da li líchnata kárta e vuv ret. [Colonel, I'm a
little worried about the ID.]

FLOSS (*to* KELIMA). He could use my handset.

NIKOLAI (*Kavkhaz*). Ne se beskpokóite. Shte gi proverím
vednága. [Don't worry. We'll check them out. I want to sort
this first.]

KELIMA (*gently*). No. It is better use his radio.

2nd KAVKHAZIAN (*Kavkhaz*). Slóusham goospoodíneh.
[Yes, sir.]

NIKOLAI. OK.

NIKOLAI *goes out. The* 2nd KAVKHAZIAN SOLDIER
goes to talk to the family, waving the 1st KAVKHAZIAN
SOLDIER *to join him.*

2nd KAVKHAZIAN (*Kavkhaz*). Dragosláv, elá e pozdraví
náshite rodníni. [Dragoslav. Come and welcome our
cousins.]

KELIMA (*to* FLOSS). And maybe now you take my young
friend Sergei to our fourwheel. He is very sick.

The BOY *doesn't look sick.*

FLOSS. He's sick?

KELIMA. Oh yes. Maybe kind UN man puts him in our
    fourwheel.

FLOSS. Why not.

She goes to LEN.

TREVELYAN. Why don't we take them all?

KELIMA. No, just the boy. I think we keep the others here.

En route to LEN, FLOSS *notices that the* KAVKHAZIAN
SOLDIERS *are talking to the family and gestures* EMELA
to try and listen in. She goes over. FLOSS *goes to the UN
soldier.*

FLOSS. Len, can we put this young man in the cruiser?

LEN. Yes, sure thing.

LEN *goes over, takes the* BOY *by the hand.*

KELIMA. Uh, no, I mean our fourwheel.

FLOSS. Our landcruiser's better. It's got air-conditioning.

LEN *takes the* BOY *out.*

Right. We should call in to our HQ as well.

JAMES *reaches for his mobile,* FLOSS *shakes her head.*

JAMES. What, you want to leave the delivery unguarded?

FLOSS. Oh, why not. After all, it seems the least of anyone's
    concerns. Trev, go and marshall everyone.

TREVELYAN. Yuh. Sure.

He goes out. JAMES *looking bemused.* EMELA *comes
forward.*

EMELA. Floss, one of the soldier speak to young man in
    wheelchair.

FLOSS. Yes?

EMELA. Soldier speak Kavkhazian.

FLOSS. Well they *are* Kavkhazian.

EMELA. I know. I just don't think they understand
Kavkhazian completely well.

FLOSS. Oh, why?

EMELA. I not so up-to-speed on Kavkhaz slang. But I think
soldier ask if he may fuck his mother.

They look over to the family just as the 2nd KAVKHAZIAN
SOLDIER *draws his weapon. The* YOUNG MAN *stands up
from the wheelchair with the pistol he has concealed
underneath the blanket, and fires at the* 2nd KAVKHAZIAN
SOLDIER, *who is shot and falls. The* 1st KAVKHAZIAN
SOLDIER *ducks behind the supplies as the* FATHER *and*
MOTHER *also produce weapons and fire.*

FLOSS. James! Emela! Get out!

FLOSS and EMELA run out the way NIKOLAI *and* LEN
went out. The family opens fire on the consignment.

JAMES *(in despair)*. Not the fucking supplies.

Blind, the 1st KAVKHAZIAN SOLDIER *shoots* JAMES
and is shot himself. JAMES *is wounded and falls. The* 1st
KAVKHAZIAN SOLDIER *falls dead behind the supplies.*
KELIMA *takes the* FATHER*'s rifle and goes over to check
that no one is returning.*

KELIMA *(Drozhdani)*. Hadi, chevik. [OK. Let's move.
Quickly!]

The MOTHER *and the* YOUNG MAN *move quickly to strip
the* KAVKHAZIAN SOLDIERS *of their weapons and
documents. The* FATHER *starts pulling out boxes from the
cube.* KELIMA *to* JAMES:

Are you OK?

JAMES. You fucking bastards. The *supplies*.

KELIMA. Where is the diamorphine?

JAMES. Surgical.

Sound of gunfire from off.

KELIMA (*Drozhdani*). Aman yarabbi, chevik ol! [Shit. Hurry!]

> *English, to* JAMES:

> And the valium?

JAMES. Diazepam. Basic Drugs kits.

KELIMA (*Drozhdani, calls*). Diyamorfini jarrahi baghlamalarda, diyazipami uyushturujular paketlerinde tapajaksiniz. [Find diamorphine in surgical kits, Diazepam in Basic Drugs.]

> *To* JAMES:

> Can I – is there anything to help?

JAMES. Well, I need something for the bleeding.

KELIMA. Uh . . .

> *She pulls her scarf off and uses it to wrap* JAMES*'s arm.* JAMES *gestures to the* FATHER *who has taken a few kits from the cube.*

JAMES. And a jab. In fact, a little morphine wouldn't go amiss . . .

KELIMA (*Drozhdani, to the* FATHER). Diyamorfini tapin! [Find the diamorphine!]

> *The* FATHER *searches as* KELIMA *continues to bind the wound:*

JAMES. There are no buses.

KELIMA. There are buses. There are no Kavkhazians.

JAMES. You could take it all.

KELIMA. We have no time.

JAMES. So you take the stuff that you can sell for arms.

KELIMA. Yes. This is a war you maybe notice.

JAMES. I notice you use kids to wage it.

KELIMA (*calls to the* FATHER, *in Drozhdani*). Paketi tap, chevik! [Find me the pack! Quickly!]

By now all the 'Kavkhazians' except the FATHER *are taking out boxes and running back for more. As the* FATHER *finds the surgical boxes and the morphine:*

Use kids as decoy. They use kids to kill.

JAMES. Oh, yuh?

KELIMA. Oh, yuh. Kids nine and ten are force to club own grandfather to death.

The FATHER *has the right pack. He is worried about the firing across his trajectory.*

JAMES. And so, what happened to the real family?

KELIMA *looks at* JAMES. *The* FATHER *calls.*

FATHER (*Drozhdani*). Hey, tutsana! [Hey! Catch.]

KELIMA *turns, the* FATHER *throws the pack, which* KELIMA *catches.*

JAMES. And for that matter, what will happen to the young boy now?

We hear the sound of helicopters. KELIMA *is tearing at the pack to get it open.*

KELIMA. Many time in war it does not always go as perfect plan.

YOUNG MAN (*calls, Drozhdani*). Helikopterlar galirlar ghaaliba. [I think that's helicopters.]

KELIMA (*Drozhdani, calls*). Bali, hamla helikopterlar, kochun! [Yes, it's helicopter gunships! Move!]

JAMES. It's the blue one. Open it.

KELIMA. Helicopter come. You want we take you with us?

The FATHER *and* MOTHER *run out with the last of the packs. The* YOUNG MAN *stands, covering* KELIMA.

YOUNG MAN (*Drozhdani*). Hadi, galirlar! [Come on! They're coming in!]

JAMES. No. Just put it there, in my bad hand.

KELIMA. Now –

JAMES. I can do it with my good hand.

KELIMA. Now I have to go.

Calls, in Drozhdani:

San koch, man indi galiram! [Go! I'm coming!]

Helicopters louder. The YOUNG MAN *runs out.*

JAMES (*with the syringe*). I can't do this.

KELIMA *doesn't know what to do. She takes out her own mobile phone.*

KELIMA. Do you know his number? Shubkin's number?

JAMES. No. Did you call him earlier?

KELIMA. Last call.

She presses the callback number from the earlier call.

Kolya. You have a seriously wounded man here. No. No, we have gone.

To JAMES*:*

Good luck.

She ends the call and runs out. The helicopters very loud, but the firing fades. JAMES *tries and fails to inject himself.* NIKOLAI *enters with his pistol and the* BOY *as a human shield.*

NIKOLAI. They are gone?

JAMES. Yes.

NIKOLAI. They leave supply.

JAMES. They leave supply. Look, I . . .

Enter FLOSS.

FLOSS. Oh my God.

NIKOLAI. Oh my God yes very much.

NIKOLAI *is pointing his pistol at* FLOSS.

FLOSS. I'm – this is terrible.

NIKOLAI. Yes, this is terrible.

JAMES. Floss I need this jab. As a matter of some urgency.

FLOSS (*to* NIKOLAI). I need / to help –

NIKOLAI. Do not Miss Florence Hazel Weatherby please take one step towards that man.

FLOSS. Why not?

NIKOLAI. Miss Weatherby you work with UN mandate.

FLOSS. Yes.

NIKOLAI. Provide humanitarian assistance. Keep security and safety for all citizen.

　　FLOSS *sees that* JAMES *is fainting.*

FLOSS. Colonel Shubkin, I must help my colleague.

NIKOLAI. Yes, but first you will help me. As you see two of my friend here are kill. No safety no security for them. And being naturally a primitive barbarian / I naturally –

FLOSS. Oh, Kolya, please . . .

NIKOLAI. I naturally believe in Bible, taking tooth for tooth and eye for eye. So which I kill. This boy or else your friend.

FLOSS. What do you mean?

NIKOLAI. One must be kill. Your call.

FLOSS. My *call*?

NIKOLAI. Your friend or this little man who maybe you think you are here to save. You choose. Your call.

FLOSS. This isn't serious.

NIKOLAI. I seem not serious?

FLOSS. Then OK. Shoot me.

NIKOLAI. No, not an option. Choose.

　　Pause.

FLOSS. Look. Look, demonstrably –

NIKOLAI *shoots the* BOY.

Oh God.

She realises:

No, don't –

NIKOLAI *shoots* JAMES. FLOSS *closes her eyes.*

NIKOLAI. You see. You may save one. But you refuse. If you
will choose one, one will be now alive. But you cannot
choose.

A mobile phone rings. It's JAMES*'s mobile.* NIKOLAI *goes
and answers it.*

Hallo? No, this is not James Neil. What must you say for
him?

Pause.

Thank you. Well no, I'm sorry. Mr Neil is dead. I have just
kill him.

He switches off the phone.

You go home now. UN declare evacuation of all NGOs. You
go, they bomb.

He tosses her JAMES*'s phone.*

I think it better. This place not for you. 'Demonstrably'.

He turns and goes out. FLOSS *goes to the* BOY, *then to*
JAMES, *to check they're dead. As she does she repeats the
ground rules of the operation.*

FLOSS. When approaching checkpoints, always turn off radio
and headlamps, turn on cabin lights. Check everyone aware
of current evacuation plan. Check waybill, packing list and
clearances for each stop at each stop. Do not forget the
emergency radio codeword. All non essential traffic must
stop when this word is used. The code is 'Gameshow'.

A helicopter above. FLOSS *looks up.*

Scene Two

*Four months later. The helicopter lands. The deck of a US
warship in the Eastern Mediterranean. There is a searail and a
bench. GINA walks on, carrying her briefcase, her suitcase
carried by a woman SAILOR from the US Navy.*

GINA. So do I meet Professor Rothman and / Mr Davis now –

*A frisbee – marked 'Property of the US Navy' – flies in at
GINA. She catches it.*

Um, I . . .

*A BODYGUARD enters, followed by an older man in
tennis clothes. The SAILOR comes to attention. The man is
YURI VASILEVICH PETROVIAN, President of the
Republic of Kavkhazia.*

YURI VASILEVICH. I am so sorry. Only in Kavkhazia. The
Presidential Bodyguard, this terrible a shot.

GINA (*what to do with the frisbee*). Um . . .

*The BODYGUARD does 'to me' gesture, and GINA tosses
him the frisbee, which he catches with some aplomb. YURI
VASILEVICH gestures that he may go and he does.*

YURI VASILEVICH (*to the SAILOR*). Thank you so much.

The SAILOR looks to GINA.

GINA. Yes, thank you.

The SAILOR puts down GINA's bag and goes.

YURI VASILEVICH. So welcome to USS Idaho, currently I
understand precisely equidistant between Karpathos and
Crete. My name is Yuri Vasilevich Petrovian. I am General
Secretary of the Democratic Socialist Alliance Party of
Kavkhazia and President of the Republic.

He puts out his hand.

GINA. Yes, I know. I'm Gina Olsson.

She shakes his hand.

YURI VASILEVICH. Ah yes. The sadly only yet so nearly but so far Agreement of Geneva. Well now we may shake our hands at last.

GINA. Very sadly in my view.

YURI VASILEVICH. It was not yet his time.

GINA. After so many unnecessary deaths, maybe now will be its time. When the game is no longer about who wins, so both sides may.

YURI VASILEVICH. Like playing frisbee.

Enter PATTERSON, *on crutches, and* TOM ROTHMAN.

Ah. The 'Men in Black'.

GINA *looks questioningly.*

There is a white one and a coloured one. They possess considerable you might say extravagant fire-power. They think anyone who is not American is from another planet.

Louder:

I am with you Miss Olsson. I think we should play both side wins. But sadly, each time we send over frisbee, our opponents send back discus. Mr Davis, Mr Rothman, please forgive me. I have appointment to play squash with your chief military attaché.

He gives a little bow to PATTERSON *and* ROTHMAN, *and turns to go.*

TOM. Well, good luck, Mr President.

YURI VASILEVICH *goes out, as* PATTERSON *whips out a notebook, writing something down before he forgets it.* TOM *comes over to* GINA.

GINA. Well, Professor Rothman.

TOM (*shaking her hand*). Technically, Mr Special Representative. Actually, Tom. I'm delighted you could make it.

PATTERSON *puts away his notebook, hobbles over.*

PATTERSON (*coming over*). So hey Gina Olsson and how's stuff with *you*?

They embrace, with a little difficulty.

GINA. I am very well. One question.

PATTERSON. I may never rollerblade again.

GINA. No, I actually meant, what you were writing down.

PATTERSON. 'We sent a frisbee, they send back a discus'.

TOM. We're collecting suspect analogies.

GINA. I beg your pardon?

PATTERSON (*reading from his little book*). 'To put the DPF in charge of the security of Kavkhazian religious sites is like employing Adolf Hitler to organise your son's bar mitzvah'.

TOM. Taste not being the strong point of the genre.

GINA. Though in this case he is presumably quite right.

Slight pause.

TOM. Yes, almost certainly.

PATTERSON. Hey, now, would you like to freshen up?

GINA. I'd like to know what you require of me. The last time I intervened in the affairs of the Kavkhazian/Drozdhan region it led to civil war.

TOM. Now, Gina, that's ridiculous.

GINA. Oh you think so?

TOM. Or else why would we deny the students and faculty of the Sorbonne your expertise and wisdom, and drag you here?

GINA *sits on the bench, opening her briefcase, and taking out papers and faxes.*

GINA. Yes, my next question.

PATTERSON *and* TOM *sit either side of her.*

TOM. Summarize the current Kavkhazian position, as you see it.

GINA. What, from the files?

PATTERSON. That's right.

> GINA *is slightly discommoded by what seems to be a test.*

GINA. Well, thanks to your bombing threat, they've actually come on quite considerably since Finland. They are offering pretty much everything except for independence.

TOM. In exchange for?

GINA. Oh . . . protection of religious sites and cemeteries, the Kavkhar minority has veto power in the regional assembly, vitally I'd say . . .

TOM. After two years of a bitter civil war.

PATTERSON. And immunity from warcrimes prosecution.

TOM. Also vitally.

GINA. Yes, well. I only receive this on the plane.

TOM. So does this provide the Drozhdans with a next best option they'd be crazy to refuse?

GINA. I would say not.

PATTERSON. Why not?

GINA. Well, as you got everybody here by threatening to bomb Kavkhazia, the Drozhdans must assume that if they hang on long enough, then you'll have to carry out your threat.

TOM. So then, no swerving there. And the Kavkhazians?

GINA. Assume you'd never do it.

TOM. So drive on.

GINA. So the issue isn't so much *their* best option.

PATTERSON. As?

GINA. As yours.

TOM. Exactly.

> GINA *shuts her case.*

GINA. So, my first question?

PATTERSON. The United States remains committed to the achievement of a peaceful, multi-ethnic, democratic future for all peoples of the Bela river basin. It does not believe it could persuade the Kavkhaz Government nor its allies nor indeed the world community that independence for Drozhdania provides a context for that aim to be achieved.

GINA. By 'world community' you mean the Russians.

TOM. Well, Kavkhazia is a former Soviet Republic. Not some collapsing federation in the nether Balkans.

PATTERSON. So in answer to your question, what we want of you is to persuade the Drozhdans of the virtue and good sense of doing what is in their ultimate best interests. And thus to finish up on what you started so propitiously at Outokumpu.

GINA. And what makes you think that I'd do any better than I did last time?

TOM. OK. We know what people say about backchannels. What happens is, you bring the guys together who are likely to discover that they share a passion for fly-fishing, Bordeaux wine or the novels of Jane Austen, and darn it you exclude and thereby stiffen up the spoilers on both sides. And there's an argument that those other guys have stuff in common too, not least an inclination towards lopping off each other's heads and sticking them on poles. And we fear it may be actually *because* they know each other that they act this way. You know, just like those scenes in Shakespeare plays where guys called towns turn out to be first cousins married to each other's sisters and no wonder what they end up doing to each other's rated R.

Pause.

But surely we don't want to think that, do we? Surely we can't believe that on the edge of Europe at the beginning of the new millennium it's impossible for people from a different ethnic origin to live together in some kind of amity? If that was true, how could we live with it?

Pause.

GINA. So the two sides are . . . completely separate?

TOM. With precedents which stretch back to the treaty of Westphalia.

PATTERSON. But unlike in 1648, you can occasionally engineer them bumping into one another in the sauna or the bar.

GINA. But they eat / separately –

TOM. From the same kitchen, but in separate messes.

PATTERSON. And sure as hell from separate menus.

GINA. And thus far you've been taking proposals from one to the other?

PATTERSON. There is a draft agreement in your pack.

GINA. I know. It wasn't clear how much has been agreed.

PATTERSON. None of it has been agreed.

TOM. Nor can it until everything's agreed.

PATTERSON. And if they don't sign up to something, here, by tomorrow night, then all bets are off, and everyone goes home.

GINA. So there's no . . . they can't take a document back to ratify?

TOM. No.

PATTERSON. Geneva, Lesson One.

GINA. And the delegations are supported from outside?

TOM. Yes, but in situ.

PATTERSON. No calling home.

TOM. No mobile phones.

PATTERSON. The Drozhdans have a former Presidential special counsel.

TOM. Very former. And not very special.

PATTERSON. And there's a guy here called Al Bek.

Slight pause.

GINA. Ah.

TOM. It was him who started the analogy collection.

GINA. Was it now. He's with the Drozhdan delegation also?

TOM. No. He's with the bad guys.

GINA. Bad guys.

TOM. And I can't believe I said that, Pat, can you?

Slight pause.

And nor can I believe I'm going to say the following, but it's the truth. You're here because two people who sincerely want to stop this nightmare feel – but cannot say – that the good guys seem at present neither smart enough nor nice enough to help.

He sees someone approaching.

I'll see you later.

He goes out. KELIMA *enters, to lean on the rail and smoke a cigarette.*

PATTERSON (*to* GINA). It wasn't wrong in principle. It was the wrong time. There is a season for all things under heaven. And we have to think, now, that the time is ripe to make a little history.

KELIMA *looks over and sees* GINA.

Of course you know Kelima Bejta. Who like every member of the Drozhdan delegation has the right of veto over all decisions. They call it 'decision-making by consensus'. We call it something else.

PATTERSON *goes out.*

GINA. Hallo.

KELIMA. I hear that you are coming.

GINA. Well, and here I am.

KELIMA. You are no longer in diplomacy?

GINA. No. I am in academia.

Slight pause.

Hasim Majdani's here?

KELIMA. He is. In fact now he high leadership.

GINA. So I understand. I'm pleased. So how / are the talks –

KELIMA. I think you know of Florence Weatherby.

GINA. Why do you mention her?

KELIMA. I see her recently.

GINA. Yes, so I heard.

KELIMA. Where we both learn that what you choose to say and do in a midst of civil war can be a matter of some consequence.

GINA. Of course. I understand that. Which is why I'm here.

KELIMA. Me also.

GINA. And because I promised you Geneva wouldn't be the end. That this would happen. That this thing would come to pass.

KELIMA. As long Miss Gina Olsson you are not here to betray us once again.

KELIMA *turns and goes quickly out.* GINA *picks up her suitcase and goes out the other way.*

Scene Three

*The next day. Night. The stateroom in which the Drozhdan
delegation meets. Maps, papers on a large table. AL BEK,
now 38, sits with his feet up on the table. GINA enters with her
briefcase and documents. She is surprised and not pleased to
see AL.*

GINA. Ah.

AL. Hey, Mohammad? Mountain.

GINA. I beg your pardon?

AL. After all, it's been all of a whole day.

GINA. The meeting starts here shortly.

AL. The meeting starts here a quarter of an hour ago. But then,
it's a meeting of the Drozhdan delegation.

GINA. I think you'll find tonight it will start shortly. There is
much to do.

AL. What, like rubberstamp the terms for our surrender?

GINA. No, to find your next and better option.

AL. Oh, yuh, that old thing.

GINA. I was surprised . . . I thought you were inclined towards
your father's side.

AL. Hey, listen. I'm a lawyer. I'm a cab. You hire me, and tell
me where you want to go.

GINA. What, they hail you first?

AL. Also I married a Kavkhaz girl.

Slight pause.

GINA. Aha.

AL. How's . . . Erik? And, uh, Jan?

GINA. Well done. Oh, Erik is just fine. He sees more of Jan
than I do, in the term time, as he lives nearby Jan's school.

AL. Aha.

GINA. And that's when I'm not in France.

AL. Oho.

GINA. And what does this, this 'Kavkhaz girl' tell you that you didn't know about your roots?

AL. A people which comes into a barren place and makes it grow. A country which is invaded and defeated and enslaved, more times that it cares to count. Which stands up when it can to outside force on behalf of, yes, actually, European values, culture, civilisation, and where it can't, which tries to keep that dream alive. And when at last it wins the right to run its own affairs, in its own way, the world turns round and calls it a pariah. And indeed claims that it stands, not for culture and enlightenment, but mediaeval barbarism. And tries to expel it from that very company of nations it has stood on Europe's outer ramparts to defend.

GINA. There is . . . is there not, something perhaps a little bit intoxicating about that story.

AL. There's something perhaps a little bit tragic / about it –

GINA. All that loss. So many times, to stand up so alone, defiant yet defeated. But actually *everybody* thinks they are the last bulwark against the bestial hordes. Everybody thinks: Beyond us, the barbarians.

AL. Especially the Finns.

GINA. Of course. Whereas in fact / if you look just to the east of Finland –

AL. Whereas in fact the Drozhdans are actually the epitome of civilised contemporary values. As they put it, if the choice is Coca-Cola or Cyrillic, we choose Coke. If it's country music or the balalaika, we'll go for Nashville every time. In fact, you could say that the Drozhdan way is US capitalism, red in tooth and claw. Strange bedfellows for you.

GINA. They're not my bedfellows.

AL. No, sure. The honest broker.

GINA. And if they are so familiar with the market system, then surely it's because they were excluded from the state one for so long.

AL. That and the fact the marketplace is where you find narcotics, arms and girls.

Slight pause.

GINA. I'm sorry, but we should not have this conversation.

AL. I'm sorry also, but not just for that.

Slight pause.

GINA. Yes, what?

AL. I gather you've been helping them to, what? – to 'focus' their demands.

GINA. I've been trying to help them put together something both sides can accept.

AL. Oh then I've got it wrong. I thought it was a test designed for us to fail.

GINA. There is no test designed for you to fail.

AL. Oh, no? Now try and see this thing the way it looks from our side. What's the deal? Essentially, devolution of the powers of government from Kavkhars to Drozhdanis. Problem: the Drozhdans don't believe that even if they cut the deal, the Khavkars will keep their side of the bargain. And the only way to guarantee that is for someone to come in and police it.

GINA. Sure.

AL. But that has problems too. One is that Petrovian won't stand for NATO crawling over sovereign Kavkhaz territory. Two is that the Americans won't stand for getting sucked into a long-term ground commitment. 'Cos even without body bags, the 82nd Airborne doesn't really want to spend the next five years patrolling buffer zones and taking kids to school. What it really wants is for Kavkhazia to be comprehensively humiliated, so to provoke the generals if not the populace to overthrow the President.

GINA. Well, good.

AL. And why would they want to do that?

GINA. Because Petrovian's a war criminal.

AL. No more than half the leaders of the world.

GINA. I would contest that.

AL. Sure. But what you can't contest is that the US has another interest in getting rid of him.

GINA. Go on.

AL. Has anybody talked about the economics of this thing to you?

GINA. What, the west wants to get its hands on a clapped-out nickel mine, some superannuated smelting plants and a mountain-full of ecologically lethal Drozhdanian brown coal?

AL. Well, don't underestimate the nickel or the coal. The world needs batteries. Drozhdevnyan power stations supply half of southern Russia.

GINA. Good for southern Russia.

AL. But the real issue is the oil.

GINA. Neither Drozhdania nor Kavkhazia have any oil.

AL. I am talking naturally about the pipeline from the Caspian which as you'll know can either run through an increasingly Islamic and anti-US Gezekhstan or through Kavkhazia and western Drozdhevnya to the sea.

GINA. I'm sorry, I'm not one for sinister conspiracies.

AL. But, Gina, you're the victim of a sinister conspiracy. Don't you understand? They've brought you here to fail. So they can say, hey, look, we did our best, we went that extra mile, hell, we even jetted in some crazy lefty Nordic feminist to have them all hear inner voices and do drums, but still the bastard wouldn't budge. And so eventually, reluctantly, they impose a US-friendly independent Drozhdan state on us from 15,000 feet.

Pause.

GINA. If that's the case, then there's an easy way to stop it.

AL. Oh?

GINA. Accept the deal.

AL. As I say, it's designed for us to fail.

PATTERSON *enters, now with one crutch, and papers.*

GINA. I don't agree.

AL. Ask yourself: What are the two things we could never do?

PATTERSON. Hi, Al.

AL. Hi, Pat.

PATTERSON. Hey, isn't this the stateroom of the Drozhdan delegation?

AL. Sure.

To GINA:

What happens is that you put two sets of people with two options in two rooms. And you have some smart guys running back and forth from room to room telling one thing to one group and another to the other. But I'm told there is one question you can ask, to find out if they're telling you the truth.

GINA. Sure. I remember. You ask them: 'If I asked you what to do – '

AL. And the liar lies about the fact he'd lie.

AL goes out. PATTERSON *gets himself to the table.*

PATTERSON. So what's the scoop?

GINA. They've not decided.

PATTERSON. I hope you underlined the overwhelming argument for swerving.

GINA. Is that really what you wanted me to do?

PATTERSON. Of course.

> PATTERSON *sees the Drozhdan delegation entering.*

I'll lead this one, OK?

> *Enter the Drozhdan delegation, which includes* KELIMA,
> HASIM MAJDANI, *the 31-year-old military leader*
> ZELIM ZAGAYEV, *his translator* EMELA, *and* LOU
> WASSERMAN, *an American lawyer in his early 50s.*

HASIM. Good evening.

PATTERSON. Hey everybody's here. Miss Olsson, I told you.
You gotta have a little faith in people.

> GINA *smiles wanly. She and* PATTERSON *sit, followed by
> the others.*

LOU. Yuh, sorry. We are fourteen minutes late.

PATTERSON. There speaks a former counsel to the United
Auto Workers. And we were a tad late too. But at least, for
all of us, that concentrates the mind.

> *This statement concentrates everybody's mind.*

For in approximately half an hour I have to take a call from
a Most Important Person and I'd really like to tell him we're
approaching closure here.

> EMELA *is whispering the translation to* ZELIM:

EMELA (*Drozhdani, to* ZELIM). Chokh muhum bir kishi zang
edajaq ona. [He has a call coming in from a VIP.]

LOU. And what Most Important Person might that be?

PATTERSON. Well, I think you've met him, Lou. As I
recollect, you've got a picture of him standing with you on
the sidewalk just outside the Waldorf on your wall.

LOU. The President.

ZELIM (*to* EMELA). Petrovian?

EMELA (*on* ZELIM's *behalf*). This is President of Kavkhazia?

PATTERSON. No, the President of the United States. Who
    calls at 4.00 pm Eastern Standard Time and to whom I
    intend to give an answer. The President of Kavkhazia is
    resident, and we can consult at any time.

> KELIMA *stands, goes and gets an empty chair, places it at
> the table and sits back in her own chair.*

> What's this?

HASIM. Ms Olsson think it good for us to have empty chair at
    table, representing President Petrovian.

PATTERSON. Ms Olsson is surely right. However, at this
    moment, I would like you to consider this.

> *He pushes the documents round the table so everyone can
> take one.*

EMELA. What is this?

PATTERSON. It's the latest draft of the agreement.

EMELA. And you like for us to consider this.

PATTERSON. Consider and agree.

> *Pause.*

HASIM. This evening.

PATTERSON. This hour.

> *Pause.*

EMELA (*Drozhdani, to* ZELIM). Bu yeni musvadda'yi bir saat
    ichariya kaabul etmamiz lazimdir. [This is the new draft for
    us to agree within an hour.]

LOU. It will be hard to do that unless it is substantially
    different from the previous document.

PATTERSON. OK. It is different in that we have firmed up –
    at your insistence – the position of the Drozhdan language
    not only in schools but in all official communications and
    government departments.

> *This line as* PATTERSON *goes on:*

EMELA (*Drozhdani, to* ZELIM). Drozhdan dil shartlari subutlandi. [The Drozdhan language provisions are firmed up.]

PATTERSON. And it is different – crucially – in that in the spirit of democracy and equal rights for all, there is no longer a Kavkhaz veto on anything in the assembly, including matters relating to government employment, education, health provision and security.

EMELA (*Drozhdani, to* ZELIM). Kavkhaz vetoso qaldirildi. [And they've removed the Kavkhaz veto.]

GINA. I'm sorry?

PATTERSON. It is different, crucially, in that in the context of democracy and equal / rights for all –

GINA. No, I heard.

PATTERSON. I'm glad, because it's what this delegation has demanded. Constantly. As it has demanded also that the jurisdiction of the International Criminal Court be guaranteed. As it now is, by insisting that the Supreme Court of Kavkhazia will . . .

He finds the place.

' . . . will place no bar to its investigations, and acknowledges a responsibility to implement its judgements fully'.

He lets this sink in for a moment, as:

EMELA (*Drozhdani, to* ZELIM). Harbi jinaayat tribunalina kaabul ettilar. [And they've given in on the warcrimes court.]

GINA. So there is no amnesty for anyone.

PATTERSON. Correct. As I say, we have been listening.

GINA. But surely/, it's impossible –

HASIM. But surely it no different in that it will not offer us independent Drozdhania.

EMELA (*Drozhdani, to* ZELIM). Madjaani bunun farq etmayajaini deyir. [Madjani says it is no different.]

ZELIM (*Drozhdani*). Ona de ki Madjaani haqlidir. [Tell him Madjani's right].

PATTERSON. No. It offers a degree – a huge degree, much greater than before – of sovereignty and autonomy. But no, not independence.

EMELA. So, Commander Zagayev says, it is not different at all.

PATTERSON. It's the same in that it denies you the right to join another state.

Impatience.

But as you have all said repeatedly that you don't wish to join another state I can't see that's a problem.

This speech underneath the following two speeches:

EMELA (*Drozhdani, to* ZELIM). Gezekhstania birlashmak istamassak problem olmayajaq deyir. [He says it's no problem unless we want to join Gezekhstan.]

LOU. Pat, that's like saying if you don't want to go abroad it doesn't matter if they take away your passport.

PATTERSON. No, it isn't, Lou, that's frankly a ridiculous analogy / and you know it –

GINA. The final difference being that it is considered by the Kavkhazian delegation as we speak.

Pause.

PATTERSON. As Ms Olsson reminds me, helpfully.

EMELA. You mean, they consider now this document?

PATTERSON. That's right.

HASIM. And will they accept it?

PATTERSON. I have no idea.

EMELA (*Drozhdani, to* ZELIM). Deyir ki Kavkharlar musvadda'yi indi teemmul edayirlar. [She says the Kavkhars are considering this now.]

KELIMA. And will they know what we decide before they do?

Slight pause.

PATTERSON. No they will not. And visa-versa, obviously.

Pause.

KELIMA. So it is possible that neither will accept this document.

PATTERSON. Clearly.

LOU. In which case, all the acronyms go home.

PATTERSON. As night follows day.

EMELA (*Drozhdani, to* ZELIM). Agar iki taraf kaabul etmassa, USA, UN va NATO gari chakajaqlar. [If neither side accepts this, the USA, UN and NATO withdraw.]

KELIMA. But it also possible for both accept. In / which case –

PATTERSON. – in which case an excellent agreement will be implemented.

No one's entirely convinced.

EMELA (*Drozhdani, to* ZELIM). Iki taraf iyi sazish kaabul edajaq. [Both sides accept a good agreement.]

PATTERSON. And obviously in theory you could say no and they could say yes.

KELIMA. In which case . . .

PATTERSON. . . . it would be hard to see a role for the international community.

LOU. You'd leave 'em to the tender mercies of the Kavkhaz Ministry of the Interior.

EMELA (*Drozhdani, to* ZELIM):Biz 'kheyr', onlar 'bali'. Muhtemel deyil. [We 'no', they 'yes'. Unlikely.]

Pause.

KELIMA. So the possibility to be considered most actually presumably is not that but the opposite. We agree and they will not.

This speech under the next two speeches:

ZELIM (*Drozhdani*). Onlara shoyle anlat. Duello yapan iki
kishi var. Takja bir tapanja dolduruldu ama hansi tabanjadir
bilmiyarlar – tetik basinjaya qadar. [Tell them the situation
is like two men who fight a duel. And they know one
pistol's loaded and one isn't. But they don't know which
until they press the trigger.]

Meanwhile:

PATTERSON. That would appear to follow.

KELIMA. And hi there B52s. And farewell President
Petrovian.

Pause.

PATTERSON. As I say, we wish both sides to go for this. But
if they don't, and you do, then they will have to think about
the consequences.

EMELA. Commander Zagayev wishes to portray this situation
as he see it. He says it like two enemies who fight a duel.
And they both know that one pistol's loaded and the other
one is not. But they don't know which until they fire.

PATTERSON. Please tell Commander Zagayev that in my
opinion he has hit the button.

EMELA *looks confused.*

That that's a very apposite analogy.

EMELA (*Drozhdani, to* ZELIM). Mejaaziniz khoshuna galir.
[He likes your metaphor.]

PATTERSON. But I would underline this fact. Whatever way
they jump, you get the legal system, fiscal policy,
employment law, schools, hospitals and police force that
you want. Without any let or hindrance. Just by signing
there.

GINA *stands, goes round to 'Petrovian's' chair, and sits in
it. As she does so:*

EMELA (*Drozhdani, to* ZELIM). Istadiyimiz kanunlar,
vergilar, tarbiya, sahiyya va polisi alabilmamizin uzerinda

durur. [He emphasises that we get the laws, taxes, education, health and police force that we want.]

But EMELA *is interrupted:*

PATTERSON. Yes, Gina?

GINA. I've a question.

PATTERSON. Mr President.

GINA. If I asked you what the hell you're trying to make me do, what would you say?

But YURI VASILEVICH *is already in the room, followed by* ROMAN *and a troubled* TOM. GINA *rises.*

YURI VASILEVICH. Well good evening Mr Patterson Davis, and distinguished members of Drozhdani delegation. Miss Olsson please do not get up. Now is this my chair?

GINA *sits.* YURI VASILEVICH *sits in what was* GINA*'s chair.* PATTERSON *looks at* TOM, *who answers the implied question with a gesture halfway between a shake and a shrug.*

Now in handbook the first thing they say is that the point of talks like these is *not* for door she suddenly fly open and behold the other side walk in the room and everything is solve. The idea indeed is quite exactly that communication goes via these good people and so to speak the medium is the messenger. Certainly this was the way of things at the Treaty of Westphalia.

He picks up a biscuit and tastes it, as:

EMELA (*Drozhdani, to* ZELIM). Iki taraf bashbasha danishmali deyir. [He says that the two sides should speak directly.]

YURI VASILEVICH. Ah you have cookies. We have cheese. When we begin, stupendous choice. Now there is only one. But I am assured it is the best.

EMELA (*Drozhdani, to* ZELIM). Biskuvit haqqinda zeraafet eder. [He jokes about the biscuits.]

YURI VASILEVICH (*standing and going round the table*). But why should I not talk direct with Commander Zagayev, who come here from his job as public gardener in Munich to lead great freedom-loving private army?

EMELA (*Drozhdani, to* ZELIM). Sizi hamla edir, ve indi mani hamla edajaq. [He is attacking you. And I think now me.]

YURI VASILEVICH. With his beautiful translator with her perfect Kavkhaz and Gezhekh, oh I am so sorry Kavkhaz and 'Drozdhanian', why should we have to talk via the diplomatic corps of the United States?

EMELA (*Drozhdani, to* ZELIM). Dediyim kimi. [As I say.]

YURI VASILEVICH. Why should I not have chat with my old friend and comrade Dr Hasim Majdani. We share many memories. Not like these bright young people for whom epoch of socialism like mediaeval times. We know about all Russian yoke.

EMELA (*Drozhdani, to* ZELIM). Sosialist era haqqinda danishir. [He talks about socialist days.]

YURI VASILEVICH. And yeah sure they are United States. If they tell us Monday's Tuesday then we must nod politely and agree. But secretly we whisper. Wednesday is today. Knowing that there is nothing in United States as old or maybe we might think as beautiful as one solitary orchard in Kavkhazia.

EMELA (*Drozhdani, to* ZELIM). Kavkhazyadaki eski baghlar haqqinda hissi danishma [Sentiment about old orchards in Kavkhazia.]

Enter AL *with a pile of papers.*

YURI VASILEVICH. And I see Mr Wasserman.

Corrects himself elaborately:

I beg his pardon *Counsel* Wasserman. But see. I have my Counsel too.

He takes the documents from AL:

There is some change. Some things they stay the same. But we word process. Nice clean copy. I am told the crucial thing in these negotiations is to understand the real interests of both side.

EMELA (*Drozhdani, to* ZELIM). Yeni bir sanad. [It's a new document.]

He distributes the documents:

YURI VASILEVICH. We want to stay one country. They want to be a country too. Maybe you expect for me to bring a sword or ploughshare but I bring something else. A pair of – how d'you say it?

He mimes scissors.

TOM. Scissors.

YURI VASILEVICH. Scissors.

EMELA (*Drozhdani, to* ZELIM). Qaychi haqqinda bir shey danishir. [It's something about scissors.]

YURI VASILEVICH (*to* PATTERSON). You should write that down.

He goes out.

PATTERSON (*to* TOM). What is it?

TOM (*to* PATTERSON). Well, you could say, they've changed their next best option. And thereby everybody else's. And thereby, the game.

EMELA (*Drozhdani, to* ZELIM). Yepyeni bir oyun. [A whole new game.]

ROMAN *sits.*

ROMAN. We are trying to address the problem of two opposites that seem irreconcilable. Our proposal has an ancient precedent. It is based on a Talmudic principle: 'Where justice prevails, there is not peace, and where peace prevails there is no justice. So where is the justice that contains peace? Indeed it is in partition'.

EMELA (*Drozhdani, to* ZELIM). Hududu dayishtirmak
istayirlar. [They are proposing to redraw the border.]

ZELIM (*Drozhdani*). Na? [What?]

ROMAN *lets it sink in.*

ROMAN. Another way of thinking is, how many problems
disappear when Basda Brod is not in Drozhdevnya but
Kavkhazia.

Referring to his copy of the document:

The border remains open to negotiation. The Bela river
forms a natural boundary for a proportion of its length.

EMELA (*Drozhdani, to* ZELIM). Hududu, chay boyuna
chizdilar. [They have redrawn the border along the river.]

ROMAN. We have drawn it obviously with our population and
religious sites on our side. Some people perhaps will wish
and need to leave their homes but we hope not too many.

EMELA (*Drozhdani, to* ZELIM). Milli tamizlama olajaq
laakin az olajaqtir. [There will be ethnic cleansing but not
too much.]

He looks round the table.

AL. In fact there's some US Air Force software we've been
playing with, which effectively maps the territory in 3-D.
You see it as if you're flying over in an airplane. So you
get a sense of natural defences, mountains, rivers and the
like.

ROMAN. And therefore what's defensible against a neighbour.
On the principle good neighbours need good walls. So
maybe you need time to read this document?

These next two speeches underneath the following four:

EMELA (*Drozhdani, to* ZELIM). Hudud bilgisayarda
chizdilar. Sanadi okhumayi istarik mi? [They have worked it
out on a computer. Do we want to read the document?]

ZELIM (*Drozhdani*). Kishidan Berushka nikeli va Agaridaki
madeni tasfiyakhaanalar haqqinda sor. [Ask him about the
Berushka nickel and the smelting plants in Agari.]

HASIM. So new Drozhdania is independent?

AL. No more or less than the United States.

HASIM. And is Estafan in Drozhdania?

ROMAN. Of course. It is a Muslim town.

EMELA. Commander Zagayev asks about Berushka nickel mine and the Atagi smelting plants.

GINA stands.

ROMAN. Gina, you want to say . . .

GINA. I'm sorry, I . . . This is quite abject. This is a betrayal. Worse, this is surrender.

ROMAN. Of what? By who?

GINA. Of the spirit of a peaceful democratic multi-ethnic state with equal rights for all.

She walks out on to the deck.

ZELIM (*Drozhdani*). Na oliyar? [What is happening?]

EMELA (*Drozhdani, to* ZELIM). Ethiraz edir ghaaliba. [I think this is a protest.]

HASIM stands.

HASIM. Please forgive me for one second.

ZELIM (*Drozhdani*). Madjaani niya chikhir? [Why is Majdani going?]

HASIM (*Drozhdani*). Miss Olsunla danishmaq istiram. [I wish to speak to Miss Olsson]. (*English.*) After all, she is why we're here.

He goes out after GINA.

AL. The answer is, that the Berushka coal field – and the nickel mines – stay in Drozdhania. Atagi on the other hand is a centre of Kavkhaz population and indeed religious sites. But all of this is subject / to negotiation –

ROMAN (*stands*). I'd suggest we all take five.

He tidies the documents in front of him.

Scene Four

Continuous. Night. GINA *on the upper deck. Enter* HASIM.

HASIM. Gina.

GINA. So what do they want? What are they saying, what are you hearing?

HASIM. I hear the Americans say 'fifteen minutes' time'.

GINA. And yet it must be the right time to ask these questions.

Enter ROMAN.

HASIM. What do they want? To cut off bits they don't want. Keep the bits they do.

GINA. Like the upper waters of the Bela River.

HASIM. We keep the nickel and the coal.

GINA. And the smelting plants and power stations?

HASIM. So we must trade.

GINA. Oh, sure. And what d'you make of 'some people will wish and need to leave their homes'?

Pause.

ROMAN. However you redraw the map, there will be mixed areas.

GINA. No, I want to hear what *he* thinks.

HASIM. Wherever you draw border there are mixed areas.

GINA. But not of course so many as there were two years ago. When Fiore-Sukhidat was a third Kavkhazi. When there was a Drozhdan population still in Novye Ghla. But more now than in two years' time. If there are any left at all.

Enter TOM *and* PATTERSON.

'Good neighbours need good walls.'

She goes down to the lower deck.

TOM. Look, I'm sorry, but time is pressing down on us.

ROMAN. Yes I know.

He goes down to the lower deck.

HASIM (*to* TOM *and* PATTERSON). I go back to talk to Zagayev.

TOM (*pats him on the arm*). Good.

HASIM *goes out.* TOM *and* PATTERSON *whisper. Below:*

GINA (*to* ROMAN, *referring to* HASIM). And what do you think Majdani wants?

ROMAN. What, generally?

GINA. Out of this – solution.

ROMAN. We know. He wants an independent state.

TOM *and* PATTERSON *have decided to follow* GINA *and* ROMAN *on to the lower deck.*

GINA. And why?

ROMAN. It's not so bad. To want to watch your flag go up at the Olympics. To receive ambassadors. To see your face on all the stamps.

TOM *and* PATTERSON *approach.*

PATTERSON. Now, guys. Forgive us, but we're going to have to ask you to postpone this conversation.

GINA. And these men from the new world and the new world order? What is in this thing for them?

TOM. Gina, this is not the time.

ROMAN. They want to make peace. It's the purpose of diplomacy.

GINA. And some people even get the Nobel prize.

PATTERSON. Yuh sure. And some get fired.

GINA. And sure they lift their sanctions and they get their pipeline and their client state . . .

TOM. Gina, if this was all about a goddamn pipeline we'd be
    dancing round the deck.

GINA. But in fact I don't think it's about these things at all.
    It's not even about punishing the Kavkhars for making you
    look stupid at Geneva or overthrowing President Petrovian.
    I think it's really just so you can say: 'We are Americans.
    We want a world where everyone will live together, across
    the ethnic divide, in peace and harmony'. Even though our
    people live in barricaded homes with armed response and
    half of the young black men in jail.

PATTERSON. Now that *is* a highly inappropriate / analogy –

GINA. And as Americans of course we must always be the
    good guys in defence of truth and justice and the right.

PATTERSON. But Gina in this case we *are* for truth and
    justice and the right.

GINA (*to* ROMAN). You see, they told me I was brought here
    to persuade you you could be the kind of people we want
    you to be. But what they really meant was: Please, become
    the kind of people we want *us* to be. Or else we'll bomb
    you all to shit until you do.

TOM. We brought you here to make a peace. Yes, what we
    wanted was to give both populations self-determination and
    a multi-ethnic liberal democracy. But it seems we can't have
    both and the alternative is neither. And surely self-
    determination's preferable to nothing, Unless anything's that
    short of everything is of no interest to you.

    During this, KELIMA *comes out of the stateroom with a
    document, and then comes down on to the lower deck.*

PATTERSON. Hey. There is a story, of a friend of ours. Who
    was faced with a bad choice – a choice she shouldn't have
    been faced with – and quite properly refused to take it. But
    unfortunately her refusal led to one and maybe two
    unnecessary deaths. And so she skulks off home to try and
    wash away her guilt at keeping her hands clean.

    Pause.

TOM. It is – of course – the next best option.

KELIMA. Oh, you think so? I think in fact it next worst thing.

PATTERSON. Ms Bejta. We are coming.

KELIMA. I am look for Gina Olsson.

TOM. Ah. I was hoping that you looked for us.

Standoff moment. PATTERSON *decides to break it.*

PATTERSON (*to* GINA). You're right. It's not the best deal. But now it's on the table every other option's worse. Not least for the Drozhdan population. So of course you will encourage Ms Bejta not to veto it. As a matter of the utmost urgency.

PATTERSON *and* TOM *go up and out.*

GINA. Well?

KELIMA *reads to* GINA*:*

KELIMA. 'The Supreme Court of the Republic of Kavkhazia accepts the jurisdiction of the International Criminal Court'.

GINA. I fear they are unlikely to accept that.

ROMAN. We did. This is our draft.

GINA (*surprised*). It is?

KELIMA. 'And will place no bar to its investigations, and acknowledges a authority to implement its judgments'.

GINA. Yes. This clause is drafted by the Americans.

KELIMA. Well, nearly.

GINA. Well, actually.

KELIMA. Except maybe for 'a authority'.

ROMAN. A missing 'n'.

He goes over to KELIMA.

I doubt we'll have to vote on it. I'll add it in myself.

KELIMA (*holding the document away from* ROMAN). Showing maybe first I think a missing word. But then I think maybe a changing word.

Slight pause.

And at first, I think it's 'obligation' but of course that too begin with vowel. Duty, maybe. I look back. It's 'responsibility'.

Pause. Roman gestures: 'So?'.

You have 'responsibility' you have to do it. You have 'authority' you do it if you like. And under nice new map, Bazarat, its bridge, its cemetery and its military policemen, all are in Kavkhazia.

Pause.

ROMAN. They are. Of course, there is / no conscious connection –

KELIMA (*to* GINA). So tell me. You who say so often, that we acknowledge and confront our past, tell me what shall I say to the mothers of the people who die there? To my mother? When those who kill so many there and elsewhere get off free. What shall I say to her?

GINA *is silent.*

ROMAN (*to* KELIMA). You tell her you have what you want. And maybe you point out that we too get to keep our monasteries and power stations but we lose our coal and nickel but more importantly our mountains, and our people die for what? And perhaps you mention that although you get your country or enough of it to call a country it may not be actually viable. And the Americans themselves don't have to bomb us or worse to police us but they're stuck with President Petrovian and I put money that their pipeline ends up running south through Gezekhstan. You tell her we are acting all of us like good Kavkhazians, quite so selfishly as possible. So how is it, she might ask, that we end up with the second worse for everyone?

Pause.

GINA. So why can't we / go back to –

ROMAN. I wanted Finland to succeed. I wanted to make history. But we find there's too much history already. And now we should both go and sign away Miss Olsson's hopes and dreams for us.

KELIMA. Of course. Miss Gina Olsson.

ROMAN. So shall we go?

KELIMA. Who is so acute at exposing everybody else's interests. But, what of hers?

GINA. What do you mean?

KELIMA. Not fame or fortune, certainly. Maybe not even Nobel Prize.

GINA. As if.

KELIMA. But something much more precious.

GINA. Yes what?

KELIMA. Her sense of worth.

Pause.

And as everybody knows, self-worth is relative. You sense it by feeling more of worth than those around you. You are first-world liberal, they are third-world tinpot dictator. You are feminist, they are all male chauvinism pigs. You are universal, they particular. You modern, and they primitive. You green, they red in tooth and claw. Not for you to be immerse in dead tradition. You have no past. They have no future.

Pause.

Or rather you are not so much bothered by your past. Family. 'Forefathers'. Tradition. Tribe. Yes, history. These matters do not interest you so much. So you forget them. And you impose your own forgetting on the world. This is message you may take back now from free Drozhdania.

ROMAN *remembers when he last heard those words.*

ROMAN. I beg your pardon?

KELIMA. I'm sorry. You have a problem with my English?

ROMAN. No. I have no problem with your English.

KELIMA. Good.

ROMAN. Miss Bejta, we did not quite make handshake in Geneva. Now we have agreement may we shake hands now?

KELIMA. 'We have agreement'.

ROMAN. Well, if you agree.

KELIMA. Well, that remain yet to be seen.

Suddenly, ROMAN *takes both of* KELIMA*'s hands.*

Uh . . .

ROMAN. Yes.

KELIMA. What's this?

ROMAN. You don't remember.

KELIMA. What should I remember?

ROMAN. Oh, chapter ten, verse 92. 'This day shall we save thee in thy body, so that thou might be a sign to those who will come after.'

GINA. What?

ROMAN. A good act. On a little patch of common ground. In defiance of our common history. I'll see you back in there.

He goes upstairs, meeting TOM PATTERSON, *and* AL, *coming back out and down to* KELIMA, *with a mobile phone.*

GINA. What does he mean?

KELIMA. I've no idea.

TOM. Miss Bejta, there's a call for you.

GINA. What, now?

TOM. Yes, now.

KELIMA. I call back.

PATTERSON. This is not that kind of call.

KELIMA *shrugs, takes the phone.*

KELIMA. Hallo.

Oh, yes. hallo.

Yes, well . . .

Yes, as you say, a compromise. In everybody's best interests. As all best compromises are.

Yes I do very much so hope so. Soon.

She holds out the phone to GINA:

He wants to speak to 'Mrs Olsson'.

GINA *shakes her head.*

No, I'm sorry. She is gone to bed. Here it is very late.

Me too.

She closes the call. She doesn't know what to do with the handset. TOM *takes it from her.*

(*To* PATTERSON.) He speak to everyone?

TOM. He speaks to everyone. And now we're nearly through.

TOM *gestures to the others to go back in.* TOM, PATTERSON *and* ROMAN *go back up and out.*

KELIMA. It is pathetic. He ask me if I will go home. I lie.

AL. Why aren't you going home?

KELIMA. I ask Ms Olsson what I should say. She has no answer. I suspect my friends who will receive no justice, I suspect they have an answer.

Slight pause.

Hey. Good real irony. If warcrime people charge your President, he is prisoner inside your country. While I am prisoner outside. My prison is the world.

She turns to go.

GINA. You let him go.

KELIMA. It was an act of weakness. As result, my sister's
death stay unavenged for ever.

Slight pause.

We are not brave enough.

GINA. For war? For peace?

KELIMA. For either.

She goes out.

AL. Who let who go?

GINA. It doesn't matter.

AL. Oh?

Pause.

GINA. Someone did the opposite of what you might expect of
them. Did something better than you might expect of them.
Someone faced with a hard choice who made a brave one.

Slight pause.

Long time ago.

*Behind them, television screens come on. Virtual reality,
three-dimensional images of the country seen from an
airplane, manipulable in three dimensions. Silhouetted
against the images are AL, HASIM, ROMAN,
PATTERSON, TOM, YURI VASILEVICH, ZELIM,
EMELA. Gradually, as the men negotiate, the light from the
televisions fades.*

HASIM. No, that's Kudjali. It's a Muslim village.

EMELA (*Drozhdani, to* ZELIM). Kudjaali Muselmandir.
[Kudjali's Muslim.]

ROMAN. Well, predominantly.

ZELIM (*Drozhdani, to* EMELA). Bela chayi mi o? [Is that the
Bela river?]

YURI VASILEVICH. OK. Left three degrees.

EMELA. Commander Zagayev asks, is that the Bela River?

ROMAN . No it's a tributary.

HASIM. And it's not defensible.

EMELA (*Drozhdani, to* ZELIM). Bu mudaafie edilmes bir
chayayaghidir. [It's an undefensible tributary.]

ROMAN. It's not a matter of defensible. It's a matter of
approachable. There is a road.

EMELA (*Drozhdani, to* ZELIM). Yol var. [The road.]

ZELIM. (*Drozhdani*): Bu asfalt edilmamish bir yol. [It's an
unpaved track.]

PATTERSON. What kind of road?

EMELA. The Commander says it's just a track. It isn't even
paved.

TOM. Easy. We'll pave it.

EMELA (*Drozhdani, to* ZELIM). Asfalt ettirajaqlar onu. [They
will pave it.]

AL. That's a monastery.

HASIM. Across the river from a mosque.

EMELA (*Drozhdani, to* ZELIM). O masjiddir. [That's a
mosque.]

PATTERSON. That's presumably a bridge?

YURI VASILEVICH. Then you blow the bridge and the river
is the frontier.

ROMAN. You can't.

EMELA (*Drozhdani, to* ZELIM). Korpuyu partlatamaslar.
[They can't blow up the bridge.]

YURI VASILEVICH . Why not?

ROMAN. You need it for the road.

Scene Five

Two years later. A hall in Drozhdania. It's threadbare and cold, and currently in darkness. FLOSS *is leading a session with a group of young people. She comes forward carrying a table and a torch.* ASLAN, *a 12-year-old Drozhdani boy, brings a plastic chair, a black rubbish bag of objects and an oil lamp.* FLOSS *puts down the table,* ASLAN *puts the chair down beside it and lights the lamp. There's an edgy, slightly threatened atmosphere from the beginning.*

FLOSS. Look, I'm so sorry. Petrol. Shall we make a start?

ASLAN (*translates into Drozhdani*). Bashlarikh. [Let's begin.]

FLOSS. Can you put the things out?

ASLAN *takes the objects out of the bag and places them on the table. They are seemingly random, mostly domestic objects: mugs, photographs, postcards, shoes, magazines and newspapers, a kite, tools, an empty but elaborately shaped duty-free whisky bottle. Once* ASLAN *has started, a door opens and shuts.* FLOSS *carries on anyway.*

FLOSS. Well, hi. Good evening. Now you'll remember last week we did the silent tableaux. The fairground and the seaside and the family meal. To start us off, could somebody describe what happened in one of them?

ASLAN (*translates into Drozhdani*). Istayir ki kimsa insan haykallardan biri tasvir esta. [She wants someone to describe one of the human sculptures.]

FLOSS. I thought the family one was particularly interesting.

ASLAN (*translates into Drozhdani*). Balka aila tablosu. [Maybe the family one.]

FLOSS. It was done three ways. In the first . . .

The lights come on. The fittings are very primitive.

Aha. The government must have paid the bill.

Lights flicker.

Or at least put something on account.

ASLAN (*translates into Drozhdani*). Hokumat balka hesaabin bahzisi odadi. [The government might have paid some of the bill.]

Hardly any laughter. She notices people she didn't expect.

FLOSS. Oh, right. I see.

Pause.

FLOSS. Well. Today I want to start with these. These are things I asked you to bring in, things that are significant to you. First, this is a woman's weekly magazine. It's German but it could be any language. It's the kind of thing that in the west you read and throw away. I wonder why it's so important to the person who brought it here.

ASLAN (*translates into Drozhdani*). Bu zhurnal niya muhum? [Why is this magazine important?]

FLOSS *waits for a response. None comes.*

FLOSS. Perhaps it would be good to remind everybody of our golden rule. Anyone who wants to, you can always leave. The door is always open.

ASLAN (*translates into Drozhdani*). Qapi daaim achiqtir, deyir. [She says: The door is always open.]

She carries on.

FLOSS. A child's sandal.

ASLAN. Sandal?

FLOSS. This kind of shoe.

ASLAN (*translates into Drozhdani*). Ushaq tuflisi. [Child's shoe.]

FLOSS. An empty whisky bottle. Tantalising.

ASLAN *looks confused.*

Um – strange. Begs questions.

ASLAN (*translates into Drozhdani*). Bosh shusha bashina dushmur. [She doesn't understand the empty bottle.]

FLOSS. I wonder . . . is the sandal, does it belong to a baby of a person here? Or someone else's baby? Or someone here when they were a baby? Maybe a sandal that a baby has outgrown. Or the sandal of a baby who will not outgrow it.

ASLAN (*translates into Drozhdani*). Ushaq tuflisi haqqinda sorushur kime aaitti filan. [She is wondering about the child's shoe and who it might have belonged to]

No reply. FLOSS *picks up a kite.*

FLOSS. And here a kite. I heard that they were banning kites. Along with audio cassettes and televisions and images of human beings and women in employment.

Slight pause.

Not that there's that much male employment since they closed the mines.

ASLAN *looks at her; she shakes her head.*

This is of course impossible. With these men here.

She shakes her head to ASLAN*; he needn't translate. Nor the following:*

But for what it's worth, the main thing I had planned to do today was to take a situation, like we did with the two young people who wanted to go out together who had problems with their parents.

A bearded PARAMILITARY *with a green headband walks from the audience on to the stage. He ignores* FLOSS *but looks at the objects on the table.*

This time I wanted to explore the situation of a small village school – this is happening, near Kudjali, which for the duration was run by, by the people who ran things at home, while the men were all away. And then a hero comes back from the war.

The PARAMILITARY *looks at* FLOSS.

... and he takes over, and he wants to change the school ...
the way it's run ... to make it more ...

Pause.

PARAMILITARY. Yes I think you know that this is not a good
idea.

Pause.

FLOSS. Well, it's not a good idea with all your people
standing round.

PARAMILITARY. 'Your people'. Where you come from?

FLOSS. London. So are you Drozhdanian?

PARAMILITARY. No. But I have been fighting for my cousins
here.

FLOSS. Fighting for what?

PARAMILITARY. For an independent country which has made
its choice.

FLOSS. Oh, you think so?

PARAMILITARY. As opposed yes to the choices you imposed
on them. Colonialism, Marxism. And now global market
place.

FLOSS. Yes of course. But does it have to be Islamic /
fundamentalism –

PARAMILITARY. So what else do you have to recommend?

FLOSS. I hear you.

Another PARAMILITARY *calls from the audience.*

2nd PARAMILITARY (*Drozhdani*). Onu khaarija tulla!
[Throw her out.]

PARAMILITARY. He thinks that you should leave.

FLOSS. Here? Or the country.

The 2nd PARAMILITARY *walks on to the stage.*

2nd PARAMILITARY (*Drozhdani*). Kifaayettir. [She's done
enough.]

PARAMILITARY. He thinks you've done enough.

FLOSS. He does?

PARAMILITARY. But in answer to your question, I am
originally from Kabul.

FLOSS looks at him.

FLOSS. Well. So you are.

She turns out front, speaking to the group.

I have abandoned people here before. I do not intend to
abandon them again.

ASLAN looks questioningly. She shakes her head.

These people want to stop the meetings. But I don't think
it's their decision.

She nods at ASLAN *to translate that.*

ASLAN (*translates into Drozhdani*). Askar gorushu sakhlamaq
istayirlar. [The soldiers want to stop the meetings.]

FLOSS. So I'm going to take a vote.

ASLAN (*translates into Drozhdani*). Sas verma istayir. [She's
going to take a vote.]

2nd PARAMILITARY (*Drozhdani*). Onlara sas mi verdirir?
[She's going to have them *vote*?]

PARAMILITARY. You know, I think they understand that it
would not be well advised to raise their hands.

FLOSS. OK. Good point. So me must find another way. I
know . . . let's say that some of you are liars. Some of you
tell truth. But only you know which you are.

ASLAN (*translates into Drozhdani*). Bahzimiz yalanja,
bahzimiz haqiqat derik. [Some of us are liars. Some of us
tell truth.]

FLOSS. Now translate this carefully. If I ask you to put up
your hands if you want me to obey these men, what would
you do?

The PARAMILITARIES *look at each other.*

Tell them.

ASLAN (*translates into Drozhdani*). Agar sizdan rijaa eder ki: alinizi qaldirin agar siz onun bu kishilari itaat etmasini istayarsaniz, na edajaqsiniz? [If she asks you to put up your hands if you want her to obey these men, what would you do?]

Silence as FLOSS, ASLAN *and the* PARAMILITARIES *watch.* FLOSS *sits and looks up at the men.*

FLOSS. You heard.

End of play.

War and Peace after the Cold War: a Selective Chronology

1989   *November:* Breaching of the Berlin Wall leads to the fall of communist governments in Eastern Europe.

1990   Secret talks between IRA and former MI6 officer.
February: Nelson Mandela released from prison.
August: Failed coup by Communist hard-liners against Mikhail Gorbachev. ANC suspends its armed struggle in South Africa.
November: Chechnya Congress declares Chechnya independent.
December: Break up of Soviet Union.

1991   *January-February:* America and its allies win the Gulf war against Iraq.
June: Slovenia secedes from Yugoslavia.
October: John Hume begins his initiative to end the war in Northern Ireland.
November: Serbia takes Vukovar in eastern Croatia.
December: Negotiations for majority rule begin in South Africa. The European Union recognises independent Croatia.

1992   *March:* Bosnia declares itself independent and Bosnian war begins.
June: Gerry Adams joins John Hume in drafting document for peace in Northern Ireland.
June: Nelson Mandela breaks off South African peace talks after 48 people are killed in township attack.
August: Torture and starvation of Muslim prisoners at Omarska concentration camp in northern Bosnia exposed.
December: ANC conducts private negotiations with Nationalist government in the South African bush.

1993   *January:* Negotiations in Geneva on Vance/Owen plan
to end Bosnian war. Secret talks between Palestinians
and Israelis begin in Norway.
March: Face-to-face meetings between British
government representatives and Sinn Fein.
September: Yitzak Rabin and Yasser Arafat sign the
Oslo agreement in Washington.
December: British and Irish governments make Downing
Street Declaration on the future of Northern Ireland.

1994   *January:* Muslim/Croat war breaks out in Bosnia.
April: ANC wins South Africa's first free elections and
Nelson Mandela becomes President.
September: IRA ceasefire in Northern Ireland.
December: Russian troops attack the Chechen capital
Grozny.

1995   *July:* Up to 8,000 Muslims massacred by Serb forces
after the fall of Srebrenica.
August: Shelling of Sarajevo market place kills 37 and
leads to NATO bombing of Serbian positions.
November: Peace talks at Dayton, Ohio, settle the
conflict in Bosnia.

1996   *February:* Palestinian suicide bombers kill 54 people
and threaten peace process.
August: Peace deal in Chechnya leads to Russian
withdrawal.

1998   *April:* Good Friday agreement in Northern Ireland.

1999   *January:* Serb paramilitaries kill 45 ethnic Albanians in
Racak, Kosovo.
February: Proximity talks to avert war in Kosovo begin
at Rambouillet in France.
March: Following the failure of the Rambouillet
negotiations, NATO begins its bombing campaign
against Serbia, leading to mass ethnic cleansing of the
Albanian population of Kosovo.
June: NATO ends its bombing campaign as Serbs
prepare to leave Kosovo and UN troops move in.

July: 13 Serb farmers are massacred in Graco, Kosovo.
October: Russian troops mount second invasion of breakway Chechen republic.
November: Power-sharing executive formed in Northern Ireland.

2000 *February:* Power-sharing executive suspended in Northern Ireland.
May: Power-sharing executive restored in Northern Ireland.
September: Ariel Sharon's visit to the Dome on the Rock in Jerusalem provokes renewed violence in Israel and Palestine.
November: Slobodan Milosevic loses Yugoslav Presidential election and is overthrown.

2001 *January:* Palestinians reject US-brokered peace deal in the dying days of the Clinton Presidency as middle east conflict continues.
March: Macedonia launches offensive against rebel Albanians seeking to divide the country along ethnic lines.
June: Opponents of the Good Friday agreement make gains in the British general election.